ENGLISH
FOR ACCOUNTING AND AUDITING

ProEnglish Publishing

ENGLISH FOR ACCOUNTING AND AUDITING
Teacher's Book

First Edition

Author
Dejan Arsenovski

Publisher
ProEnglish Publishing

Design and Prepress
Vesna Pijanović

Illustrations Credits
Andrey_Popov, www.shutterstock.com

ISBN 978-86-921225-2-1

© 2019 All rights reserved

No part of this book may be reproduced or transmitted in any form or by any means, electronic or mechanical, including photocopying, recording or by any information storage or retrieval system, without the permission of the publisher.

Dejan Arsenovski

ENGLISH
FOR ACCOUNTING AND AUDITING

Teacher's Book

PROENGLISH PUBLISHING

Table of Contents

A GUIDE TO THE BOOK	**6**

UNIT 1
Accounting Sectors — 8

- Reading 1: Accounting Career — 8
- Focus on vocabulary: Collocations — 10
- Focus on grammar: Mixed Tenses — 11
- Reading 2: Accounting Jobs — 12
- Writing task — 13
- Building up a new vocabulary — 13

UNIT 2
Accounting Essentials — 14

- Reading 1: Key Accounting Terms — 15
- Focus on vocabulary: Prepositions — 17
- Focus on grammar: Present Simple Tense — 17
- Reading 2: Types of Business Organisations — 18
- Writing task — 19
- Building up a new vocabulary — 19

UNIT 3
Accounting Cycle — 20

- Reading 1: Accounting Cycle — 21
- Focus on vocabulary: Understanding Closing Procedures — 22
- Focus on grammar: Past Simple Tense — 23
- Reading 2: Year-End Closing Procedures — 23
- Writing task — 24
- Building up a new vocabulary — 25

UNIT 4
Costs Vs Expenses — 26

- Reading 1: Types of Costs — 27
- Focus on vocabulary: Presenting Your Figures — 29
- Focus on grammar: Present Continuous Tense — 29
- Reading 2: Recording Expenses — 29
- Writing task — 31
- Building up a new vocabulary — 31

UNIT 5
Profit and Loss Account — 32

- Reading 1: Revenues and Expenses Vs Gains and Losses — 33
- Focus on vocabulary: Income Statement Entries — 34
- Focus on grammar: Past Continuous Tense — 35
- Reading 2: P&L Account Format — 35
- Writing task — 37
- Building up a new vocabulary — 37

UNIT 6
Balance Sheet — 38

- Reading 1: Balance Sheet Components — 39
- Focus on vocabulary: Accounting Synonyms — 42
- Focus on grammar: Present Perfect Tense — 42
- Reading 2: Fundamental Analysis — 43
- Writing task — 44
- Building up a new vocabulary — 45

UNIT 7
Cash Flow Statement — 46

- Reading 1: Cash Flow Statement — 47
- Focus on vocabulary: Small Talk — 48
- Focus on grammar: Present Perfect Continuous — 49
- Reading 2: What is Equity? — 49
- Writing task — 50
- Building up a new vocabulary — 51

UNIT 8
Taxation — 52

- Reading 1: Key Taxation Terms — 52
- Focus on vocabulary: Tax Collocations — 55
- Focus on grammar: Going to + Infinitive for Future Predictions — 55
- Reading 2: Types of Taxes — 55
- Writing task — 57
- Building up a new vocabulary — 57

UNIT 9
Accounting Department   **58**

Reading 1: Payroll   59
Focus on vocabulary: Procurement Terms   61
Focus on grammar: Present Continuous for Future Arrangements   61
Reading 2: Cash Collection, Cash Disbursement and Procurement   62
Writing task   64
Building up a new vocabulary   65

UNIT 10
Guiding Principles of Accounting   **66**

Reading 1: IFRS   66
Focus on vocabulary: Global Financial Reporting Language   68
Focus on grammar: Passive Voice   69
Reading 2: Fundamental Accounting Principles   69
Writing task   71
Building up a new vocabulary   71

UNIT 11
Corporate Crime and Internal Controls   **72**

Reading 1: Accounting Fraud   73
Focus on vocabulary: Types of Corporate Crimes   76
Focus on grammar: First Conditional   76
Reading 2: Internal Control   77
Writing task   78
Building up a new vocabulary   79

UNIT 12
Accrual Basis Accounting   **80**

Reading 1: Accrual-Basis Accounting   81
Focus on vocabulary: Accrual-Basis Accounting Key Terms   82
Focus on grammar: Second Conditional   83
Reading 2: Timing Differences   83
Writing task   85
Building up a new vocabulary   85

UNIT 13
Depreciation   **86**

Reading 1: Depreciation Key Facts   86
Focus on vocabulary: Depreciation Key Terms   89
Focus on grammar: Obligation, Permission, Lack of Obligation   89
Reading 2: Calculating Depreciation   89
Writing task   91
Building up a new vocabulary   91

UNIT 14
Intangible Assets   **92**

Reading 1: Classification of Intangible Assets   92
Focus on vocabulary: Intangible Assets Key Terms   94
Focus on grammar: Modals of Probability   95
Reading 2: Valuation of Intangible Assets   95
Writing task   96
Building up a new vocabulary   97

UNIT 15
Auditing   **98**

Reading 1: Audit Procedures   98
Focus on vocabulary: Auditor's Terminology   100
Focus on grammar: Reported Speech   101
Reading 2: Audit Report   101
Writing task   103
Building up a new vocabulary   103

Extra Activities   **104**
Extra Activities: The Key   **144**
Collocation Bank   **162**
GLOSSARY   **166**

A Guide to The Book

UNIT PATTERN

1. READING SECTION 1
2. FOCUS ON VOCABULARY
3. FOCUS ON GRAMMAR
4. READING SECTION 2
5. WRITING TASK*
6. BUILDING UP A NEW VOCABULARY*

NOTE: *Writing Task* and *Building up a New Vocabulary* Section should be assigned for homework.

1. READING

Starting with *Introduction* and concluding with *Speaking Activity*, this Section provides the context, the target vocabulary and the opportunity for practice.
This Section should be presented in the following order:

1. Introduction
2. Reading Text
3. Reading Comprehension
4. Speaking

2. FOCUS ON VOCABULARY

This Section examines a specific vocabulary topic by presenting the concept in the first part and providing the opportunity for practice in the *Language Task* Section.

1. Focus on Vocabulary
2. Language Task

3. FOCUS ON GRAMMAR

This Section contains a controlled speaking activity aimed at revising grammar topics in accounting context.

4. WRITING TASK

A writing task based on a unit topic, assigned for homework.

5. BUILDING UP A NEW VOCABULARY

A term-definition matching exercise that summarises the essential unit vocabulary, assigned for homework.

UNIT 1

UNIT MAP

Reading 1: Accounting Career
Reading 2: Accounting Jobs
Focus on Vocabulary: Collocations
Language Task: Accounting Tasks
Focus on Grammar: Mixed Tenses
Writing Task: Obtaining a CPA Licence

Extra Activity 1: Gap Filling *(see page 104)*
Extra Activity 2: Rank the Skills and Qualities *(see page 104)*
Extra Activity 3: English Analysis *(see page 104)*

1. INTRODUCTION TO THE UNIT

Understanding issues dealt with in Unit 1 does not require a specialist accounting knowledge. The Unit covers topics such as reasons for choosing an accounting career, educational requirements, professional licences, accounting sectors and accounting jobs. The principal aim of the Unit is to introduce the basic accounting vocabulary and gradually lead students into more advanced accounting issues.

Note: In this Unit exceptionally, the class can begin by **Focus on Grammar Section**, a mixed-tense exercise in which students create their own professional profiles. This will give them a chance to learn about each other and revise basic grammatical structures, while you will have an opportunity to find out more about their abilities.

2. READING 1: Introduction

Note: Go through the introductory questions below and explore the topic extensively before reading the Text 1. The answers in italics are given for reference purposes and might not always coincide with the answers your students provide. Follow suit for Reading 2.

1. Why do people choose a career in accounting?
   Possible answers: *A good pay, excellent job opportunities, possibility of promotion, etc.*

2. What are the educational requirements for becoming an accountant?
   The answers vary according to national requirements.

3. What professional licences are available to accountants?
   Accountants: Certified Public Accountant (USA) or Chartered Accountant (UK);
   Auditors: Certified Auditor.

4. In what different accounting sectors can accountants pursue their career?
   In public, corporate or government accounting sector.

5. What do public accountants do?
   They work as external accountants, providing accounting services to public at large.

6. What is the difference between a public and a corporate accountant?
   Unlike public accountants who operate as external accountants, corporate accountants work as internal employees within a single company.
   Note: *corporate accounting may also refer to a branch of accounting which deals with accounting for companies.*

7. What do government accountants do?
   They maintain and examine records of government agencies, manage state and local revenues, perform compliance and financial audits of state and local-government entities.

8. What do external auditors do?
   They inspect companies' accounting records and express an opinion as to whether financial statements are presented fairly in accordance with applicable accounting standards.

9. What do internal auditors do?
   They work within an organisation and are responsible for evaluating accounting processes, risk management and internal controls.

3. READING COMPREHENSION 1: Answers

1. **Why does pursuing an accounting career provide diverse job opportunities?**
   Because accounting has always been considered the language and the basic tool of business.

2. **Why do accountants obtain professional licences?**
   The licence demonstrates that they have undergone further training and examination, proving to their clients that they possess a high level of professional competence.

3. **What is the difference between public and corporate accountants?**
   Unlike public accountants, corporate accountants work as internal employees within a single company. They are employed on a full-time basis by a company and provide accounting services for their employers exclusively.

Unit 1

4. **What do government accountants do?**
They maintain and examine records of government agencies, manage state and local revenues, perform compliance and financial audits of state and local-government entities.

Note on assurance: The aim of assurance in accounting is to enhance the reliability of information and provide users with a broader picture of the reporting entity, enabling decision-makers to make more informed and better decisions.

READING 1 KEY VOCABULARY

job security	educational requirements	bachelor's degree
professional licence	CPA	chartered accountant
public accountant	corporate accountant	internal employee
compliance and financial	audit	state and local revenues

4. SPEAKING 1

Students provide answers based on the local circumstances.

5. FOCUS ON VOCABULARY: Collocations

Explain the concept of collocations, stress their importance for language acquisition and provide examples. Ask students to identify some collocations in Reading 1.

1. hold	A. a professional licence
2. undergo	B. training
3. pursue	C. a career
4. implement	D. accounting policies
5. record	E. financial data
6. perform	F. audits
7. utilise	G. tax incentives
8. post	H. entries into the General Ledger
9. generate	I. profit
10. incur	J. losses

6. LANGUAGE TASK: What do accountants do?

1. prepare	A. financial statements
2. maintain	B. financial records
3. interpret	C. financial information to management
4. manage	D. tax issues
5. analyse	E. a company's financial position
6. advise	F. clients on how to invest money
7. fill in	G. tax returns
8. review	H. compliance with policies, procedures and laws
9. audit	I. accounts for errors, misinformation and fraud
10. oversee	J. budget and financial management

This is an excellent opportunity for students to talk about themselves and use the target vocabulary. Let them speak freely and do not overcorrect.

7. FOCUS ON GRAMMAR: Mixed Tenses

As previously mentioned, this exercise can be a fine introduction to your first class. After completing the interviews, students should be able to create their own professional profiles and present themselves in a proper manner. Students work in pairs interviewing each other. After the interview, they report information on their partner. Before starting with the pair work, make sure that students know how to form the questions properly. Check the understanding of structures, if necessary.

Sample Questions:

1. **Company:** What company do you work for?
2. **Position:** What position do you hold in the company?
3. **Department:** What department do you work in?
4. **Responsible for:** What are you responsible for?
5. **Job involves:** What does your job involve?
6. **Time with the company:** How long have you been with the company?
7. **Work experience:** How much work experience have you got?
8. **Qualifications:** What qualifications have you got?
9. **Professional Aspirations:** What are your professional aspirations?

Unit 1

8. READING 2: Introduction

Discuss different jobs that accountants do and what each particular job involves. Ask students to describe functions they perform. Take into consideration that the real life scenario might differ from the descriptions in Reading 2. Large companies may employ accountants highly specialised in one field (accounts receivable officer, accounts payable officer, payroll clerk, etc.), whereas in small companies one accountant may assume several different roles.

9. READING COMPREHENSION 2: Answers

1. **What do financial accountants do?**
   They prepare financial statements based on a company's financial records. In addition, they review financial records to ensure that they accurately reflect the operating results of a company.

2. **How do tax accountants help their clients?**
   They help their clients fill in tax returns, ensure that taxes are paid properly and on time and help clients manage tax issues.

3. **How do internal auditors assist management?**
   They assist management in improvement of risk management and internal controls.

4. **What tasks does a management accountant's work involve?**
   It involves an analysis of a company's financial position in order to provide an insight into its business performance.

READING 2 KEY VOCABULARY

advisory role	financial statements	to review financial records
operating results	to interpret accounting data	to fill in tax returns
tax compliance	tax optimisation	mergers and acquisitions
business performance	to monitor spending	budget estimate
annual budget	forensic accountant	white-collar crimes
expert witness	in-depth review	compliance with policies
internal control	material misstatement	fraud
controller		

10. SPEAKING 2

Let students speak freely and do not overcorrect.
Additional idea: After finishing Extra Activity 2 you may ask students to write a job advertisement for an accounting or auditing position and find the most suitable candidate in the class.

11. WRITING TASK

Assign the Writing Task for homework.

12. BUILDING UP A NEW VOCABULARY

1. Chartered Accountant	A. an accountant who has passed the professional examinations administered by a country's Institute of Chartered accountants
2. Public Accountant	B. an accountant who provides services to public at large
3. Corporate Accountant	C. an internal company accountant
4. Financial Accountant	D. an accountant who controls the day-to-day financial management of an organisation
5. Tax Accountant	E. an accountant who help clients complete their tax returns and manage their tax issues
6. Internal Auditor	F. an internal employee of a company responsible for providing objective evaluation of the company's operations
7. External Auditor	G. an accounting professional who performs a thorough review of a company's accounting records, not employed by the company
8. Management Accountant	H. an accountant who provides the key financial information to management to help them make business decisions
9. Budget Analyst	I. an accountant who prepares budget, examines budget estimates and monitors spending
10. Controller	J. a senior accountant responsible for all accounting operations of an organisation

UNIT 2

UNIT MAP

Reading 1:   Key Accounting Terms
Reading 2:   Types of Business Organisations
Focus on Vocabulary: Prepositions
Language Task: Bookkeepers Vs Accountants
Focus on Grammar: Present Simple Tense
Writing Task: Describing Professional Functions

Extra Activity 1:   What functions do you perform? *(see page 105)*
Extra Activity 2:   Analysing Different Aspects of Business Organisations *(see page 105)*
Extra Activity 3:   Setting up a Business *(see page 105)*

1. INTRODUCTION TO THE UNIT

In the first part, Unit 2 introduces the basic accounting terms, with the definitions provided in the Reading Section. The second part of the Unit focuses on different types of business organisations, their key characteristics and the concept of liability for debts.

2. READING 1: Introduction

There are a large number of questions to start the lesson with. Choose the questions according to the abilities of your class.

1. What information is recorded in accounting records?
   Accounting records contain information on a company's transactions.

2. Where do accountants first record business transactions?
   They are first recorded in journals.

3. In which accounting records are transactions subsequently posted?
   They are subsequently recorded in the general ledger.

4. What term describes the process of transferring transactions into journals and ledgers?
   Posting or recording transactions.

5. What term describes the written form of a recorded transaction?
   An entry.

6. How are different groups of transactions classified?
   They are classified into different accounts.

7. What is a list of all company's accounts called?
   A chart of accounts.

8. In what order are the accounts presented in a chart of accounts?
   Balance sheet accounts are listed first, followed by income statement accounts.

9. How many accounts can a company's chart of accounts include?
   Depending on the size of a company, a chart of accounts may list as few as thirty accounts or as many as thousands.

10. In how many accounts is each transaction recorded?
    In at least two accounts: one account is debited and the other account is credited.

11. Why is each transactions recorded in at least two accounts?
    Because this complies with the basic rule in accounting which states that all debits must equal credits.

12. What are the specific rules or principles that an entity follows when preparing its financial statements?
    Accounting policies.

3. READING COMPREHENSION 1: Answers

1. **What tasks do accountants perform?**
   They are responsible for keeping or maintaining, preparing, examining, inspecting and interpreting a company's financial records.

2. **What is a chart of accounts?**
   A listing of all accounts used in the general ledger of an organisation.

3. **How are transactions recorded under the double-entry bookkeeping system?**
   Each transaction is recorded in at least two accounts, which means that each transaction has an appropriate debit and credit entry.

4. **What are accounting policies?**
   Accounting policies are specific rules, principles and procedures used and consistently followed by a company to prepare and report its financial statements.

READING 1 KEY VOCABULARY

financial records	transaction	journal
ledger	entry	chart of accounts
balance sheet	income statement	double-entry bookkeeping
debit entry	credit entry	accounting policy
accounting practice	financial statements	

4. SPEAKING 1

Students provide answers based on their company's practice.

5. FOCUS ON VOCABULARY: Prepositions

Point out that in verb-preposition or adjective-preposition combinations, corresponding prepositions must be learnt by heart.

Note: 'responsible' collocates both with *for* and *to*, depending on the context.

1. responsible	A. for
2. specialised	B. in
3. deal	C. with
4. in charge	D. of
5. entitled	E. to
6. comply	F. with
7. related	G. to
8. advise	H. on
9. exempt	I. from
10. subtracted	J. from

6. LANGUAGE TASK: Bookkeepers Vs Accountants

1. **Bookkeepers** record financial transactions.
2. **Accountants** are responsible for preparing tax returns.
3. **Accountants** analyse financial data.
4. **Bookkeepers** maintain general ledgers.
5. **Accountants** prepare financial statements.
6. **Accountants** interpret financial data to the company management.
7. **Bookkeepers** post journal entries.
8. **Bookkeepers** produce invoices.
9. **Accountants** are in charge of establishing and monitoring control procedures.
10. **Bookkeepers** post debits and credits.

7. FOCUS ON GRAMMAR: Present Simple Tense

Students use the Unit vocabulary to form questions about the routine activities they perform.

Unit 2

8. READING 2: Introduction

Discuss different considerations to be taken into account before forming a company, as presented in Reading 2 (formation expense, management simplicity, liability for debts, tax considerations, etc.). In a stronger class, ask students to explain the differences between different forms of business organisations.

9. READING COMPREHENSION 2: Answers

1. **What factors should be considered before establishing a business organisation?**

   The expense of forming and operating the business, management simplicity, tax considerations, the level of control over the company's affairs, the ability to raise capital, the extent of liability for the organisation's debts.

2. **What is the difference between unincorporated and incorporated entities?**

   Unincorporated entities are those with no legal difference between the owner and the entity, while incorporated businesses are those organisations which are separate legal entities from their owners.

3. **What is the difference between a general and limited partnership?**

   The general partnership is a type of business where both partners share the profits and liabilities equally. The limited partnership is a business organisation with both general and limited partners.

4. **Why might owners of private limited companies decide to go public?**

   They decide to go public in order to raise extra capital.

READING 2 KEY VOCABULARY

entrepreneur	to set up	liability for debt
unincoporated	incorporated	sole proprietorship
self-employed	to establish	governmental interference
liable to	to incur	general partnership
limited partnership	to assume debts	private limited company
to exceed	public limited company	to raise capital
to go public	to float the company	stock exchange

10. SPEAKING 2

Let students speak freely and do not overcorrect.

11. WRITING TASK

Assign the writing task for homework.

12. BUILDING UP A NEW VOCABULARY

1. transaction	A	a business event that has a monetary impact on an entity's financial statements and is recorded as an entry in its accounting records
2. journal	B	the book of original entry
3. general ledger	C	the book of final entry
4. financial records	D	formal documents representing the transactions of a business, individual or other organisation
5. debit entry	E	an accounting entry that results in either an increase in assets or a decrease in liabilities on a company's balance sheet
6. credit entry	F	an accounting entry that either increases a liability or decreases an asset on a company's balance sheet
7. double entry bookkeeping	G	a system of accounting in which every transaction has a corresponding positive and negative entry
8. liability	H	legal responsibility for something
9. unincorporated entity	I	a business organisation that does not possess a separate legal identity from its owner(s)
10. incorporated entity	J	a business organisation viewed as a separate entity from its owners

UNIT 3

UNIT MAP

Reading 1	Accounting Cycle
Reading 2	Year-End Closing Procedures
Focus on Vocabulary	Understanding Closing Procedures
Language Task	Interviewing a Candidate
Focus on Grammar	Past Simple Tense
Writing task	A Year-End Closing Checklist
Extra Activity 1	Verb-Stress Pattern *(see page 106)*

1. INTRODUCTION TO THE UNIT

> Unit 3 continues to explore the basic accounting functions. It analyses what happens from the moment of recording a transaction to the final stage of its processing – the inclusion in financial statements. In the second part, Unit 3 focuses on the year-end closing procedures - the set of activities aimed at preparing accounts for the coming year.

2. READING 1: Introduction

Try to reconstruct the entire accounting cycle process with students by asking the questions below:

1. What it is the first step in processing financial information?
   Gathering source documents and recording transactions.

2. What activities does the initial recording of financial information involve?
   - *Analysing (or examining) transaction and deciding what accounts will be affected.*
   - *Deciding what account will be debited and what account will be credited.*
   - *Documenting the transaction in a journal.*

3. How do accountants check whether the debit side total is equal to the credit side total?
   They prepare a trial balance.

4. What is an unadjusted trial balance?
   A list of account balances in general ledger at the end of a reporting period, before any adjusting entries are made to the balances.

5. What do accountants do after an unadjusted trial balance is prepared?
   They make adjusting entries.

6. What are adjusting entries?
   They are journal entries usually made at the end of an accounting period to allocate income and expense to the period in which they actually occurred.

   Note: Adjusting entries are analysed in more depth in subsequent units.

7. What document is prepared after adjusting entries are made?
   An adjusted trial balance.

8. What is an adjusted trial balance?
   A list of the balances of ledger accounts created after the adjusting entries are made and posted to ledger accounts.

9. What is the next step after preparing an adjusted trial balance?
   Organising accounts into financial statements.

10. What is the final step in processing financial information?
    Closing the books.

11. What does closing the books involve?
    Transferring balances from temporary accounts to a permanent account.

Unit 3

3. READING COMPREHENSION 1: Answers

1. **What does the term 'accounting cycle' refer to?**
   It refers to series of steps in recording an accounting event from the time a transaction occurs to its inclusion in financial statements.

2. **What is the first step in recording a business transaction?**
   Gathering source documents and recording transactions.

3. **What is an unadjusted trial balance?**
   A list of account balances in general ledger at the end of a reporting period, before any adjusting entries are made to the balances.

4. **Why are adjusting entries made?**
   To allocate income and expense to the period in which they actually occurred.

READING 1 KEY VOCABULARY

accounting cycle	accounting event	closing the books
source documents	bank statement	deposit slip
cash receipt	cash register	purchase order
employee time cards	unadjusted trial balance	correcting entry
adjusting entry	adjusted trial balance	temporary accounts
permanent accounts	business performance	

4. SPEAKING 1

Students provide answers based on their company's practice.

5. FOCUS ON VOCABULARY: Understanding Closing Procedures

1. **Checking every individual stock item:**
   Physically counting inventory

2. **Making a list of all account balances in general ledger before any adjusting entries are made:**
   Preparing an unadjusted trial balance

3. **Making a list of all company accounts that will appear on financial statements:**
   Preparing an adjusted trial balance

4. **Transferring balances from temporary to permanent accounts:**
   Closing the books

5. **Correcting misplaced decimals:**
   General error correction

6. **Comparing two sets of accounts to ensure that the balances are in agreement:**
   Reconciling accounts

7. **Placing an entry under a correct account:**
   Classification error correction

8. **Removing data from the company file:**
   Purging information that is no longer needed

6. LANGUAGE TASK: Interviewing a Candidate

A speaking exercise designed to reinforce the Unit vocabulary and improve fluency.

7. FOCUS ON GRAMMAR: Past Simple Tense

A combined grammar-vocabulary exercise designed to review the use of Past Simple Tense. After completing the exercise students report information on their partners.

8. READING 2: Introduction

1. How often do accountants perform end-of-period procedures?
   Monthly, quarterly, half-annually, annually.

2. What term is used for the end-of period procedures performed at the end of a fiscal year?
   Year-end closing procedures.

3. Why do accountants perform year-end closing procedures?
   To ensure that their accounting records are accurate, prepare a company file for the coming year and enable preparation of accurate financial statements.

4. What operations do year-end closing procedures involve?
   They involve closing the books, carrying forward balances from the previous year and opening posting accounts for the upcoming year.

5. What does the term 'reconciling accounts' mean?
   Comparing two sets of accounts to ensure that their balances are in agreement.

6. How do accountants reconcile accounts?
   By double-checking ledger entries.

7. Name some examples of reconciling company records with source documents.
   Possible answer: *Comparing bank accounts with bank statements, general ledger entries with sub--ledger entries.*

Unit 3

9. READING COMPREHENSION 2: Answers

1. **Why do companies perform year-end closing procedures?**
   To ensure that their accounting records are accurate, prepare a company file for the coming year and enable preparation of accurate financial statements.

2. **What steps do the 'year-end closing procedures' include?**
   Reconciling company files with source documents, counting inventory, checking for errors, purging information no longer needed, recording adjusting entries, organising accounts into financial statements and closing the books.

3. **What are 'closing entries'?**
   Closing entries are journal entries used to empty temporary accounts at the end of a reporting period and transfer their balances into permanent accounts.

4. **What is the difference between temporary and permanent accounts?**
   The permanent account balances are carried over to the following year, while the temporary account balances are not.

READING 2 KEY VOCABULARY

end-of-period procedures	year-end closing procedures	to carry forward balances
to reconcile accounts	physical count	inventory
purging information	closing entry	temporary accounts
permanent accounts	general error correction	classification error correction

10. SPEAKING 2

Let students speak freely and do not overcorrect.

11. WRITING TASK

Assign the writing task for homework.

12. BUILDING UP A NEW VOCABULARY

1. year-end closing procedures	A	preliminary steps taken before preparation of financial statements
2. source document	B	the original record of a transaction
3. unadjusted trial balance	C	the listing of general ledger account balances at the end of a reporting period before any adjusting entries are made
4. adjusting entry	D	journal entries made at the end of the accounting period to allocate revenue and expenses to the period in which they actually are applicable
5. carry forward	E	move to a later accounting period
6. reconcile accounts	F	compare accounts to ensure that figures are in agreement
7. inventory	G	stock
8. temporary accounts	H	accounts whose balances are not carried over from one accounting period to another
9. permanent accounts	I	accounts that are not closed at the end of accounting period
10. closing entry	J	a journal entry made at the end of an accounting period to transfer temporary accounts to permanent accounts

UNIT 4

UNIT MAP

Reading 1	Types of Costs
Reading 2	Recording Expenses
Focus on Vocabulary	Presenting Your Figures
Language Task	Describing a Line Graph
Focus on Grammar	Present Continuous Tense
Writing Task	Describing Typical Costs
Extra Activity 1	Identify the Cost *(see page 107)*
Extra Activity 2	Check Your Figures *(see page 108)*

1. INTRODUCTION TO THE UNIT

> The first part of Unit 4 focuses on the difference between costs and expenses, two related concepts with different meaning in accounting. In addition, two forms of cost classification are presented, mainly with a view to providing an overview of various individual costs.
>
> The second part of Unit 4 looks into different types of expenses, viewed as a category reflected in Profit and Loss Account, a financial statement analysed in the following Unit.

2. READING 1: Introduction

Tell students that their company is going to launch a new product. Ask the following questions:

1. How would you determine the price of a product? What information would you need?
   Possible answers: *How much customers are willing to pay; how much the competition is charging; how much profit they want to make; the break-even point; the amount of costs involved in manufacturing and advertising the product;*

Lead the conversation towards various costs that companies incur.

2. Ask students to name different costs that companies incur.
   Let students provide as many examples as possible. Possible answers: *Raw materials, labour, shipping, warehousing, administrative salaries, bonuses, commissions, advertising, legal fees, accounting fees, corporate entertainment, travel expenses, rent, lease, utilities, etc.*

3. What costs does your company incur?
   Students provide answers based on their company's business activities.

4. How can costs be classified?
   There are many different ways to classify costs, depending on the purpose of classification. This Unit deals with the direct/indirect and the fixed/variable cost classification.

5. What are direct costs?
   Costs that can be easily associated with the product being manufactured.

6. What are the examples of direct costs?
   Direct labour, raw materials, etc.

7. What are indirect costs?
   Costs that are not directly related to making a product or service. They affect the entire company, not just one product.

8. What are the examples of indirect costs?
   Advertising, depreciation, legal and accounting fees, bank charges, etc.

9. Ask students to think of a specific company and illustrate its direct and indirect costs.

10. What are fixed costs?
    Costs incurred regardless of the level of production.

11. What are the examples of fixed costs?
    Rent, utilities, insurance, etc.

12. What are variable costs?
    Costs that change with the level of output (production).

13. What are the examples of variable costs?
    Raw material, packaging, labour costs, shipping costs, etc.

14. Ask students to think of a specific company and illustrate its fixed and variable costs.

Unit 4

15. What is the difference between costs and expenses?
    Cost is the amount of cash paid to acquire a product. Expense is the part of the cost used in the process of generating revenue. Expenses only occur when the product is sold.

16. How are costs recorded in accounting records?
    They are recorded as assets on balance sheet until they are used to generate revenue.

17. When does a cost convert into an expense?
    When the related revenue is recognised.

3. READING COMPREHENSION 1: Answers

1. **What is the difference between cost and expense?**
   Cost is the amount of cash paid to acquire a product. Expense is the part of the cost used in the process of generating revenue.

2. **How are costs classified according to traceability?**
   According to traceability, they are divided into direct and indirect costs.

3. **What costs are easily associated with the product being manufactured?**
   Direct costs.

4. **How are costs classified based on their relation to change in volume?**
   They are classified as fixed and variable.

READING 1 KEY VOCABULARY

direct costs	indirect costs	raw materials
direct materials	direct labour	direct overheads
legal fees	bank charges	client entertainment
cost allocation	fixed costs	variable costs
insurance	utilities	output
packaging	labour costs	shipping costs

4. SPEAKING 1

Students provide answers based on their company's circumstances.

5. FOCUS ON VOCABULARY: Presenting Your Figures

Presenting figures effectively is an essential part of accountants' work. Use this Section to identify any gaps in your students' knowledge and help them fully master the ability to talk about figures.

1. Check your students' knowledge of cardinals, ordinals, decimals and fractions.
   Use Extra Activity 2 for further practice.
2. Make sure that students understand the meaning of the verbs/adverbs describing movement.

6. LANGUAGE TASK: Describing a Line Graph

Students use the vocabulary from the Focus on Vocabulary Section. After finishing the task, they compare the graphs to determine how accurate their descriptions are.

7. FOCUS ON GRAMMAR: Present Continuous Tense

The exercise focuses on the use of the Present Continuous Tense for current projects. Emphasise the 'around now' concept. To illustrate this, you may start by asking students to talk about their current activities: *What are you currently working on?*

8. READING 2: Introduction

Note: The income statement format will vary according to the complexity and the type of a company's business activities. The classification presented below appears in a manufacturing company's income statement.

1. Under which two categories are expenses organised within an income statement?
   - *Cost of Goods Sold*
   - *Selling, General and Administrative Expenses.*
2. What does the income statement item Cost of Goods Sold refer to?
   It refers to the direct expenses related to producing goods or rendering services.
   Note: Despite its name, 'Cost of Goods Sold' is actually an expense.
3. What are the components of Cost of Goods Sold?
   Raw materials, labour, etc.
4. What items do Selling Expenses include?
   Sales commissions, travel expenses, client entertainment, warehousing, shipping, etc.
5. What items do General and Administrative Expenses include?
   Administrative salaries and wages, executive salaries, legal fees, utilities, rent, insurance, external audit fees, etc.

Unit 4

6. Ask students to think of a specific company and illustrate its expenses as they appear in income statement. Alternatively, they can think of an imaginary company, describe its activities and illustrate the expenses.

7. How are unpaid expenses treated in accounting?
   They are recognised in full, irrespective of whether payments have been made or not.

8. Under what account are goods bought on credit recorded?
   They are recorded under the Accounts Payable account.

9. Under what account is income tax due within one year recorded?
   It is recorded under the Income Tax Payable account.

10. Under what account are expenses incurred, but not yet paid and for which an invoice has not been received recorded?
    They are recorded under the Accrued Expense account.
    Note: Accrued Expenses are analysed more extensively in Unit 12.

11. Ask students to provide examples of accrued expenses.
    Possible answers: *Salaries payable, interest payable, etc.*

9. READING COMPREHENSION 2: Answers

1. **How are expenses classified in income statement?**
   Under two categories: Cost of Goods Sold and Selling, General and Administrative Expenses.

2. **What are examples of selling expenses?**
   Sales commissions, travel expenses, client entertainment, warehousing, shipping, etc.

3. **What accounts do unpaid expenses include?**
   Accounts Payable, Income Tax Payable and Accrued Expenses.

4. **What are accrued expenses?**
   It is an account for recording expenses that have been incurred, but not yet paid and for which an invoice has not been received.

READING 2 KEY VOCABULARY

cost of goods sold	selling expenses	general and administrative expenses
sales commissions	warehousing	wages
executive salaries	shipping	utilities
research and development	severance pay	sick leave pay
accounts payable	income tax payable	accrued expense
short-term liability	tax authorities	invoice

10. SPEAKING 2

In light of Reading 2, students should focus on the fact that some expenses may not have been recorded at the end of accounting period; therefore, there is a need to update accounts, that is, to assign expenses to the appropriate accounting period.

11. WRITING TASK

Assign the writing task for homework.

12. BUILDING UP A NEW VOCABULARY

1. manufacturing costs	A	costs of all resources consumed in the process of making a product
2. operating costs	B	costs incurred in carrying out a company's day-to-day activities, but not directly associated with production
3. direct costs	C	costs that can be accurately traced to a cost object with little effort
4. indirect costs	D	costs which cannot be accurately attributed to a specific cost object
5. fixed costs	E	costs that do not vary in the short term. irrespective of changes in production or sales levels
6. variable costs	F	costs that vary depending on a company's production volume
7. warehousing	G	the process of storing goods in a warehouse
8. shipping	H	the process of transporting goods
9. income tax payable	I	an account for recording taxes that must be paid to the government within one year
10. severance pay	J	compensation paid to employees upon termination of employment

UNIT 5

UNIT MAP

Reading 1	Revenues and Expenses Vs Gains and Losses
Reading 2	P&L Account Format
Focus on Vocabulary	Income Statement Entries
Language Task	Users of Financial Statements
Focus on Grammar	Past Continuous Tense
Writing Task	Describing Income Statement Format and Content
Extra Activity 1	Income Statement Entries *(see page 109)*
Extra Activity 2	Preparing an Income Statement *(see page 110)*
Extra Activity 3	Various Expenses *(see page 110)*

1. INTRODUCTION TO THE UNIT

Unit 5 begins the analysis of primary financial statements by examining profit and loss account (also referred to as income statement, statement of operating results, etc.). The first part of the Unit focuses on the difference between revenues and expenses and gains and losses.

The second part of the Unit examines the income statement concept and format, as well as the common income statement accounts. As their number in large companies may exceed one thousand, it is impossible to encompass all entries.

2. READING 1: Introduction

Start the discussion by examining different ways in which companies earn money, steering it into direction of different types of revenues and gains.

1. In what different ways can companies earn money?
   By selling goods or rendering services, selling assets other than inventory, renting property, trading securities, lending money to other companies, etc.

2. Ask students to think of a specific company and illustrate its core and peripheral activities.

3. What is the revenue earned from a company's core (primary) operations called?
   Operating revenue.

4. What are the common examples of operating revenue?
   Money earned through sale of goods or rendering services.

5. What are the expenses incurred through a company's core operations called?
   Operating expenses.
   Note: Sometimes 'operating expenses' are considered only those expenses incurred in carrying out an organisation's day-to-day activities, but not directly related to production.

6. What are the common examples of operating expenses?
   Direct material, direct labour, rent of production facilities, shipping, etc.

7. What are the common examples of non-core activities?
   Depending on a company's main activity, they might refer to leasing property, lending money, trading securities, etc.

8. What are the examples of non-operating revenue?
   Interest earned from an investment; income earned from renting property, etc.

9. What are the examples of non-operating expenses?
   Interest paid on money borrowed, expenses incurred due to a lawsuit (i.e. solicitor's fees, legal fees)

10. How does a company record a sale of an asset other than inventory?
    It records a gain.

11. What happens if a company loses money as a result of a write-off, or negative outcome of a lawsuit?
    The company incurs loss.

12. Ask students to think of a specific company and illustrates its core and peripheral activities, operating revenue and expenses, gains and losses.

3. READING COMPREHENSION 1: Answers

1. **What is non-operating revenue?**
   Income earned through a company's non-core activities.

2. **What are non-operating expenses?**
   Expenses incurred for reasons not related to a company's normal business operations.

3. **What is the key difference between Income Statement and Balance Sheet?**
   Unlike Balance Sheet, which reflects a static position at a point in time, Profit and Loss Account reflects all transactions that have occurred during an accounting period.

4. **What are the main components of Income Statement?**
   Revenues from primary activities; Expenses from primary activities; Revenues from secondary activities; Expenses from secondary activities; Gains; Losses

READING 1 KEY VOCABULARY

profit and loss account	operating revenue	operating expenses
non-core activities	non-operating activities	non-operating expenses
gains	losses	acquisition price
write-off	lawsuit	foreign currency translation
primary activities	secondary activities	long-term assets

4. SPEAKING 1

Students provide answers based on their company's business activities.

5. FOCUS ON VOCABULARY:

Note: Answers may differ depending on a company's core activity.

Sales Revenues: OR
Costs of Goods Sold: OE
Direct Labour: OE
Selling, General and Administrative Expense: OE
Depreciation Expense: OE
Service Revenue: OR
Loss from a lawsuit: L
Cost of Material: OE
Extraordinary Losses L

Negative effects of FX translations L
Sale of Discontinued Operations G
Interest Revenue: NOR

Note: An extraordinary item is an expense or revenue item characterised by both its unusual nature and infrequency of occurrence, for instance, losses caused by flood, fire, etc. Sale of discontinued operations refers to a sale of business component.

6. LANGUAGE TASK: Users of Financial Statements

Let students discuss the reasons freely and do not overcorrect.

7. FOCUS ON GRAMMAR: Past Continuous Tense

Although the focus of the exercise is on the Past Continuous Tense, encourage students to ask additional questions using other tenses. This will give them a chance to develop fluency, practice other structures and make exercise more dynamic and natural.

8. READING 2: Introduction

Note: As the format and content of income statements vary with the needs of users, instead of asking introductory questions, you may ask students to provide as much information as possible on content, format and entries of income statements they have examined.

1. What information does a profit and loss account start with?
   Sales Revenue (Total Sales).

2. What is the final information in a profit and loss account?
   Net Income (Net Earnings, Bottom Line).

3. How do we arrive at the income statement's bottom line?
   By deducting operating expenses necessary for earning revenue from sales revenue.

4. What do the format and the content of an income statement depend on?
   They depend on complexity and type of a company's business operations. (They are different for a trading company, a service company or a manufacturing company).

5. What are the main expenses that a manufacturing company incurs?
   Cost of material used in creating the good and the direct labour cost, i.e. Cost of Goods Sold.

6. What is the amount obtained called when the Cost of Goods Sold is deducted from the Sales Revenue?
   Gross Margin.

7. What other expenses do manufacturing companies incur?
   Expenses incurred in operating a business, which are not directly associated with production of goods, i.e. Selling, General and Administrative Expense.

8. What are the examples of Selling Expenses?
   Sales person salaries and commissions, advertising and marketing, promotion materials, travel expenses, corporate entertainment, etc.

9. What are the examples of General and Administrative Expenses?
   Executive salaries, office lease and utilities, insurance, legal fees, accounting fees, consulting fees, office supplies, etc.

10. What term describes the amount obtained when Selling and Administrative Expenses are deducted from Gross Margin?
    Operating Margin.

11. What item is deducted from Operating Margin to arrive at Net Income (Net Earnings)?
    Taxes.

12. Are all net earnings distributed to shareholders?
    No. Most of them are usually reinvested into a company (retained earnings).

13. What does the income statement tell to its users?
    It tells whether the company made or lost money, whether it is spending too much on certain expenses. In addition, it allows comparison with previous years and similar businesses in the industry.

14. What is a combined income statement of a parent company with its subsidiaries called?
    Consolidated Income Statement.

9. READING COMPREHENSION 2: Answers

1. **What information does the income statement start with?**
   Sales Revenue (Total Sales).

2. **How do we arrive at the income statement's bottom line?**
   By deducting expenses from the total revenue.

3. **What is a consolidated income statement?**
   A combined income statement of a parent company with its subsidiaries.

4. **What information does EPS (earnings per share) report?**
   It tells how much money shareholders would receive if a company decided to distribute all of the net earnings for the period.

Profit and Loss Account

READING 2 KEY VOCABULARY

total sales	deductions	net income
gross margin	operating margin	parent company
subsidiary	consolidated income statement	earnings-per-share
outstanding share	common stock	retained earnings

10. SPEAKING 2

Students provide answers based on their company's business activities. Alternatively, they may report on companies they have audited or whose accounts they have examined.

11. WRITING TASK

Assign the writing task for homework.

12. BUILDING UP A NEW VOCABULARY

1.	Operating Revenue	A	income derived from sources related to a company's everyday business operations
2.	Non-Operating Revenue	B	income that results from incidental (secondary) business activities
3.	Gain	C	an increase in owner's equity resulting from a sale of an asset other than inventory
4.	Acquisition Price	D	the price that was actually paid for an asset when it was first acquired
5.	Costs of Goods Sold	E	direct costs attributable to the production of the goods sold by a company
6.	Gross Margin	F	the difference between total revenue and cost of goods sold
7.	Selling, General and Administrative Expenses	G	expenses outside of the manufacturing function
8.	Comparative Income Statement	H	a financial report that presents the results of multiple accounting periods in separate columns
9.	Consolidated Income Statement	I	a financial report prepared for a group of enterprises and its parent company as a whole
10.	Earnings Per Share	J	net income of a firm divided by the number of its outstanding shares or the shares held by the shareholders

UNIT 6

UNIT MAP

Reading 1	Balance Sheet Components
Reading 2	Fundamental Analysis
Focus on Vocabulary	Accounting Synonyms
Language Task	Balance Sheet Entries
Focus on Grammar	Present Perfect Simple Tense
Writing Task	Importance of Balance Sheet for Investors and Shareholders
Extra Activity 1	Determining a Company's Assets and Liabilities *(see page 111)*
Extra Activity 2	Interviewing a Candidate *(see Student's Book, page 114)*

1. INTRODUCTION TO THE UNIT

> Having learnt about a company's revenues and expenses, shareholders and investors need to know what the company owns and owes. This information is reported in balance sheet, another essential tool in examining a company's financial health.
>
> The first part of Unit 6 focuses on balance sheet accounts (assets, liabilities, equity), while the second part of the Unit analyses the importance of balance sheet for shareholders and investors through its role in fundamental analysis.

Balance Sheet

2. READING 1: Introduction

1. Use the example below to introduce the key balance sheet components: assets, liabilities and equity. Tell students they are going to start a small business. Their financial situation is presented below:

   You have €500 in savings. You need €1,500 to buy the equipment. You borrow €1,000 from the bank to buy the equipment. Ask the following questions:

   - *How much are your total assets worth?*   *(€1,500)*
   - *How much are your liabilities worth?*   *(€1,000)*
   - *How much is your equity worth?*   *(€500)*

   In a stronger class, you may ask students to describe balance sheet items and format for companies they have audited or whose business records they have examined.

2. What financial statement provides information on assets, liabilities and shareholders' equity?
   Balance sheet.

3. Ask students to define assets.
   Any item of economic value owned by an individual or business entity.

4. Ask students to name different types of assets.
   Cash; land; buildings; equipment; inventory; accounts receivable; intangible assets, etc.

5. How are assets classified on the balance sheet?
   They are classified into current and non-current assets (or long-term and short-term assets).

6. What are current assets?
   Assets that are easily converted into cash within one year.

7. What are the examples of current assets?
   Cash, marketable securities, accounts receivable, prepaid expenses, etc.

8. What are non-current assets?
   Assets that are not expected to became cash within one year.

9. What are the examples of non-current assets?
   Fixed assets, long-term investments, intangible assets, etc.

10. What are fixed assets?
    A category of non-current assets, reported under the category Property, Plant and Equipment in balance sheet.

11. What are liabilities?
    Money owed to lenders and suppliers, etc.

12. How are liabilities classified on the balance sheet?
    They are classified into current (short-term) and non-current (long-term) liabilities.

13. What are current liabilities?
    Debts due within a year.

Unit 6

14. What are the examples of current liabilities?
    Accounts payable, short–term loans, interests, payroll, tax, etc.

15. What are non-current liabilities?
    Debts due after a year.

16. What are the examples of non-current liabilities?
    Long-term debts, mortgage loans or bank loans with a maturity date after one year from the balance sheet date, etc.

17. Ask students to think of a specific company and illustrates its assets and liabilities.

18. A company has a possible obligation that may or may not occur depending on the outcome of a future event. How does the company reflect this event in its financial statements?
    By recording a contingent liability.

19. Where is a contingent liability recorded?
    A contingent liability is not recognised in balance sheet. However, it is disclosed in notes to financial statements.

20. What are typical examples of contingent liabilities?
    A lawsuit against an entity, when the outcome of the lawsuit is uncertain.

21. A company has an obligation that is uncertain in timing or amount. How does the company reflect this in its financial statements?
    By recording provisions.

22. What is a provision?
    It is an amount put aside to cover future liability of uncertain timing or amount.

23. What are typical examples of provisions?
    A warranty obligation, a bad debt, inventory obsolescence, a loss making contract, etc.

24. What is the third component of a balance sheet?
    Shareholders' equity.

25. What is a shareholders' equity?
    The book value of the business, i.e. the difference between the amount of assets and liabilities.

26. What is the difference between the owner's equity and the shareholders' equity?
    The term owner's equity is used on a sole proprietor's balance sheet, while the term shareholders' equity is used for companies owned by shareholders.

27. Who are the possible users of balance sheet information?
    Shareholders, management, creditors, bankers, current and potential investors, suppliers and employees.

Additional Idea – Pairwork: Student A writes the name of a person he or she knows. Student B asks questions about the person's assets, liabilities, and their net worth.

3. READING COMPREHENSION 1: Answers

1. **What are current assets?**
   Assets that are easily converted into cash within one year.

2. **What are fixed assets?**
   A category of non-current assets, reported under the category Property, Plant and Equipment in balance sheet.

3. **What are current liabilities?**
   Debts due within a year.

4. **What is the difference between owner's equity and shareholders' equity?**
   Owner's equity is the term used on a sole proprietor's balance sheet, while incorporated companies owned by shareholders use the term shareholders' equity instead.

READING 1 KEY VOCABULARY

shareholders' equity	owner's equity	accounts receivable
current assets	non-current assets	fixed assets
inventory	marketable securities	prepaid expenses
intangible assets	current liabilities	non-current liabilities
accounts payable	payroll	mortgage loan
maturity date	contingent liabilities	provisions

4. SPEAKING 1

Students provide answers based on their company's circumstances. Alternatively, they may report on companies they have audited or whose accounts they have examined.

5. FOCUS ON VOCABULARY: Accounting Synonyms

1. revenue	income
2. profit and loss account	income statement; statement of operating results; statement of earnings
3. balance sheet	statement of financial position
4. net profit	net income; net earnings; bottom line
5. inventory	stock
6. book value	carrying value
7. turnover	total sales, total revenue
8. equity	net worth
9. shareholder	stockholder
10. gearing	leverage

6. LANGUAGE TASK: Balance Sheet Entries

Provisions	L	Interest Receivable	A
Inventory	A	Bank Loans	L
Goodwill	A	Securities	A
Accounts Receivable	A	Income Tax Payable	L
Accounts Payable	L	Interest Payable	L
Cash on Hand	A	Current Account	A
Employee Benefits	L	Accrued Wages and Salaries Payable	L

7. FOCUS ON GRAMMAR: Present Perfect Simple Tense

This Section reviews the use of Present Perfect Tense in the 'recent completed activity' context.

Extra Activity 2 provides an opportunity for practising a different aspect of the use of the Present Perfect Tense, focusing on experiences taking place at an unspecified time in the past: *Have you ever....?*

8. READING 2: Introduction

1. Tell students to think of themselves as potential investors. A friend of theirs has a company that needs additional capital, while they have a certain amount of surplus funds they would like to invest. Ask what information they would like to obtain about their friend's company.
   Possible answers: *Is the business profitable? Is the company's revenue growing? Is the company able to repay its debts? How does a company's performance compare with its competitors?*

2. As a potential investor, what information can you obtain from the balance sheet?
   Information on assets and liabilities; how much debt a company has; whether a company is able to repay its debts; how much cash it needs to collect from customers; how much cash and cash equivalents it possesses, etc.

3. How can an investor learn whether a company is able to repay its short-term debts?
   By comparing current assets to current liabilities. The amount obtained when current liabilities are deducted from current assets is called working capital ratio.

4. Is the high amount of working capital always a good thing?
   Not necessarily. It could indicate that a company has too much inventory or is not investing its excess cash.

5. How can an investor learn how the company is financed, i.e. to what extent a company's operations are funded by borrowing?
   By comparing shareholders' equity to total liabilities. The amount obtained when total liabilities are divided by shareholders' equity is called debt-to-equity ratio.

6. What does this ratio identify?
   It identifies the companies that are highly leveraged and therefore a higher risk for investors.
   Note: Leverage is the amount of debt used to finance a company's assets. A company with significantly more debt than equity is considered to be highly leveraged.

7. How do investors estimate the value of the stock they want to buy?
   By performing a fundamental analysis.

8. What is the fundamental analysis?
   An evaluation of a company's stock based on the examination of a company's financial statements.

9. What does the fundamental analysis attempt to ascertain?
   It attempts to ascertain whether stock is overpriced, underpriced or priced in proportion to its market value.

9. READING COMPREHENSION 2: Answers

1. **Why is the balance sheet important for potential investors?**
   Because it tells a lot about a company's fundamentals – how much debt a company has, how much it needs to collect from customers, how much cash it has, etc.

2. **What is the fundamental analysis?**
   The analysis designed to provide an evaluation of a company's stock based on examination of a company's financial statements.

3. **What question does the working capital ratio answer?**
   Whether a company has enough short-term assets to cover its short-term debts.

4. **What is gearing?**
   A degree to which a company's operations are funded by borrowing.

READING 2 KEY VOCABULARY

fundamental analysis	company's stock	security valuation
overpriced	underpriced	growth potential
working capital	debt-to-equity ratio	gearing
comparative balance sheet		

10. SPEAKING 2

Part 1. Companies engage in financial gearing for a number of reasons. However, the most common scenario is that a company needs to raise an extra cash, but it cannot, (or does not want), to do it by selling additional shares.

Part 2. Students provide answers based on their company's circumstances. Alternatively, they may report on companies they have audited or whose accounts they have examined.

11. WRITING TASK

Assign the writing task for homework.

12. BUILDING UP A NEW VOCABULARY

1. current assets	A balance sheet accounts that represents the value of all assets that can be converted into cash within one year
2. liquid	B easy to sell or convert into cash
3. marketable securities	C very liquid securities that can be converted into cash quickly at a reasonable price
4. fixed assets	D an asset that is not consumed or sold during the normal course of business
5. accounts receivable	E money owed to a company by its debtors
6. accounts payable	F money that a company owes to its creditors
7. shareholders' equity	G a company's total assets minus total liabilities
8. fundamental analysis	H a method of security valuation which involves examining the company's financials and operations
9. working capital ratio	I a liquidity ratio that measures a company's ability to pay off its current liabilities with current assets
10. gearing	J the amount of money a company has borrowed compared to its share capital

UNIT 7

UNIT MAP

Reading 1	Cash Flow Statement
Reading 2	Statement of Changes in Equity
Focus on Vocabulary	Small Talk
Language Task	Entertaining a Client
Focus on Grammar	Present Perfect Continuous
Writing Task	Describing Sources of Cash Inflow and Outflow
Extra Activity 1	Why Small Businesses Fail *(see Student's Book, page 115)*
Extra Activity 2	Cash Flow Problems *(see page 112)*
Extra Activity 3	Shareholders' Equity *(see page 112)*

1. INTRODUCTION TO THE UNIT

> Being profitable according to accounting standards and having enough cash are not always one and the same. To find out how much money a company actually has at its disposal, owners need to look into Cash Flow Statement, the financial statement examined in the first part of Unit 7.
>
> What impact does a company's financial performance have on the value of its shares? The answer to this question lies in Statement of Changes in Equity, another component within the set of primary financial statement, analysed in the second part of Unit 7. Notes to financial statements, whose aim is to provide additional information, not included in financial statements, are also examined in this part of the Unit.

2. READING 1: Introduction

1. What information does the cash flow statement show to its readers?
   A company's cash inflows and cash outflows.

2. Why is there a need for the cash flow statement?
   The income statement uses the accrual basis accounting method, which records revenues and expenses when they are incurred, regardless of when cash is exchanged. The cash flow statement identifies the timing differences between earning income and cash collection.

3. What might be the result of not having the information provided in the cash flow statement?
   Without the information provided in the cash flow statement, a company profitable according to accounting standards may go bankrupt because it does not have enough cash to service its debts.

4. What different sources of revenue are analysed in the cash flow statement?
   Cash flow from operating activities, investing activities and financing activities.

5. What does the 'cash flow from operating activities' section show?
   How much cash the company generated from its core business.

6. What are the examples of cash inflow from operating activities?
   Cash collected from customers.

7. What are the examples of cash outflow from operating activities?
   Salaries or cash paid to suppliers.

8. What does the 'cash flow from investing activities' section show?
   The amount of cash spent on investments in assets.

9. What are the examples of cash inflow from investing activities?
   A disposal of a long-term asset.

10. What are examples of cash outflow from investing activities?
    An acquisition of a long-term asset.

11. What does the 'cash flow from financing activities' section show?
    External activities a company performs to raise capital and repay investors.

12. What are the examples of cash inflow from financing activities?
    Cash generated from the issue of shares.

13. What are the examples of cash outflow from financing activities?
    Payment of dividends or repayment of debt.

14. What it the bottom line in the cash flow statement?
    Net Increase/Net Decrease in Cash.

15. How can the information from the cash flow statement be used to determine a company's ability to service its loans?
    Through comparison of cash generated to outstanding debt.

16. Ask students to think of a specific company and illustrates its cash inflows and outflows.

Unit 7

3. READING COMPREHENSION 1: Answers

1. **Why is there a need for a cash flow statement in addition to an income statement?**
   Because it identifies the timing differences between earning income and making cash collections.

2. **What are the examples of cash inflow generated from investing activities?**
   The cash generated from a disposal of long-term asset.

3. **What are the examples of cash inflow generated from financing activities?**
   The cash generated from the issue of shares.

4. **What does the operating cash flow ratio report?**
   It tells how well current liabilities are covered by cash flow generated from a company's operations.

READING 1 KEY VOCABULARY

cash inflow	cash outflow	to generate cash
timing differences	net increase or decrease of cash	peripheral activities
disposal of asset	acquisition of asset	to raise capital
issue of shares	repayment of debt	transparency
to service loans	operating cash flow ratio	outstanding debt

4. SPEAKING 1

Students provide answers based on their company's circumstances. Alternatively, they may report on companies they have audited or whose accounts they have examined.

5. FOCUS ON VOCABULARY

Ask students if they have been in a situation to entertain a client. Ask them to provide examples and relate their experiences. Suggested safe-topic answers include: *journey; accommodation; local town; local food; sightseeing; family; holidays; free time activities; sports;* etc. Introduce the conventional phrases, such as:

> *Did you have a good journey?*
> *What was the weather like when you left?*
> *What do you think of the food here?*
> *What's your hotel like?*
> *Is this your first visit here?*
> *Have you had time for sightseeing?*

Cash Flow Statement

6. LANGUAGE TASK

Let students act out their roles freely and do not overcorrect.

7. FOCUS ON GRAMMAR

The exercise is designed to provide a natural context for the use of Present Perfect Continuous Tense.

8. READING 2: Introduction

1. Who are the main users of information reported in the Statement of Changes of Equity?
   Owners and investors.

2. What information does this financial statement disclose?
   How the equity reported in balance sheet changes over the accounting period.

3. What is the starting information in the Statement of Changes in Equity?
   It begins with the shareholders' equity shown on the balance sheet at the end of the previous year (closing balance).

4. What are the most common causes of changes in equity?
   Issue of new share capital; payment of dividends; purchase or sale of treasury stock; effects of foreign exchange transactions.

5. Why is there a need for Notes to Financial Statements?
   They provide additional information that is not included in other statutory financial statements.

6. What are the main disclosures contained in Notes to Financial Statements?
   Information on the basis for preparation of financial statements and a summary of significant accounting policies used.

7. What other disclosures do Notes to Financial Statements include?
   Information on contingent liabilities; unrecognised contractual liabilities; non-financial disclosures related to an entity's financial risk management; judgements the management has made; key assumptions about the future; other estimations used; etc.

Unit 7

9. READING COMPREHENSION 2: Answers

1. **What information does the Statement of Changes in Equity report?**
   It tells its users about the value of equity at the beginning of an accounting period and how it has changed during the year.

2. **How does it help users of financial statements?**
   It helps them identify the factors that cause a change in the equity over an accounting period and make financing decisions based on this information.

3. **What are the main causes of changes in equity?**
   Issuing new shares; generating earnings and not paying them as dividends (retained earnings); incurring trading losses; paying dividend to shareholders; purchase or sale of treasury stock; effects of foreign exchange transactions.

4. **What type of disclosures do Notes to Financial Statements include?**
   The information about the basis for preparation of financial statements and a summary of significant accounting policies used.

READING 2 KEY VOCABULARY

equity	share capital	stock corporation
public limited company	opening balance	closing balance
retained earnings	additional paid-in capital	trading losses
dividends	treasury shares	foreign exchange translation
disclosures	estimates	judgements

10. SPEAKING 2

Have students talk about different causes of changes in equity and how they would affect their investment. Alternatively, they may report on statements of changes in equity of companies they have audited or whose accounts they have examined.

11. WRITING TASK

Assign the writing task for homework.

12. BUILDING UP A NEW VOCABULARY

1. Cash Flow Statement	A	a financial report that describes the sources of a company's cash and how that cash was spent over a specified period of time
2. Cash Inflow	B	money received by an organisation as a result of its operating, investment and financing activities
3. Cash Outflow	C	the amount of cash that a company disburses
4. Operating Cash Flow Ratio	D	a measure of how well current liabilities are covered by the cash generated from a company's operations
5. Operating Activities	E	activities related to a company's core business activities, such as manufacturing, distributing, marketing and selling a product or service
6. Financing Activities	F	activities a company performs to raise capital and repay investors
7. Investment Activities	G	activities a company performs to acquire or sell assets
8. Stock Corporation	H	a company in which capital is contributed by shareholders and divided into shares
9. Treasury Shares	I	an entity's own repurchased shares
10. Foreign Exchange Translation	J	the process of restating foreign currency accounts of subsidiaries into the reporting currency of the parent company

UNIT 8

UNIT MAP

Reading 1	Key Taxation Terms
Reading 2	Types of Taxes
Focus on Vocabulary	Tax Collocations
Language Task	Collocations Applied
Focus on Grammar	Going to + Infinitive
Writing Task	Tax Report
Extra Activity 1	Creating More Effective Tax Strategy *(see Student's Book, page 119)*
Extra Activity 2	Describing Taxable Event *(see Student's Book, page 121)*
Extra Activity 3	Doing Business in Your Country *(see Student's Book, page 122)*

1. INTRODUCTION TO THE UNIT

> Unit 8 is focused on tax accounting, one of the most complex but at the same time the most important branches of accounting. A fully comprehensive analysis of this field of accounting would require far more than one unit (see ***English for Tax Professionals*** by the same author), which is why the main aim of this lesson is to present the essential tax accounting vocabulary, without touching upon the questions such as the difference between financial and tax accounting or calculation of taxable income.
>
> The first part of the Unit covers the key tax accounting terms, while the second part examines the difference between direct and indirect taxes and lists the main forms of taxes.

2. READING 1: Introduction

1. What type of services do tax accountants offer to their clients?
   Completing tax returns, ensuring tax compliance, implementing tax planning strategies, tax consulting services, preparation of tax due-diligence reports, etc.

2. What government authority is in charge of implementing tax laws and collecting taxes?
   Tax administration (tax authorities).

3. What official form do taxpayers use to declare liability for tax?
   Tax return.

4. What type of general information must be supplied in a company's tax return?
   General company information, such as full business name, registered office address, company registration number, tax identification number (UK: unique taxpayer reference), type and status of a company (holding company/ subsidiary), predominant activity, etc.

5. What is the basis for calculation of income tax?
   Taxable income.

6. How is taxable income determined?
   By subtracting various allowable deductions from the gross income.

7. Is all taxpayer's income subject to taxation?
   No, part of it is tax free.

8. What term describes the amount of income that is not subject to taxation?
   Tax allowance (UK: personal allowance).

9. How can the amount subject to taxation be reduced?
   By claiming tax deductions.

10. What is the basis for claiming tax deductions?
    Business-related expenses.

11. What organisations might be exempt from paying tax?
    The tax exempt status is usually granted to non-profit organisations, i.e. charitable, religious and educational organisations.

12. What organisations in your country are exempt from paying tax?

13. What is the general term for various tax incentives offered by governments, commonly used to attract foreign investors or to promote a certain policy?
    Tax reliefs.

14. What other incentives reduce the amount of tax paid?
    Governments may offer tax credits, which reduce the actual amount of tax owed.
    Note: the term tax credit may also refer to a sum that can be offset against a tax liability, i.e. the prepaid amount that can be deducted against the tax liability.

15. Why do governments offer tax credits?
    To promote a specific behaviour or help disadvantages taxpayers.

16. What is the difference between tax deductions and tax credits?
    Deductions reduce the amount of taxable income, while tax credits reduce the actual amount of tax owed.

17. What happens when a taxpayer pays too much tax?
    They are entitled to claim a tax refund (tax rebate).

18. What term describes the total amount of tax that an entity or individual is legally obligated to pay?
    Tax liability.

19. How is tax liability determined?
    By applying a tax rate to a tax base.

3. READING COMPREHENSION 1: Answers

1. **What type of general information must be supplied in a tax return?**
   General company information, such as full business name, registered office address, company registration number, tax identification number (UK: unique taxpayer reference), type and status of a company (holding company/ subsidiary), predominant activity, etc.

2. **How is the amount of taxable income determined?**
   By subtracting various deductions from gross income.

3. **Why do governments introduce tax reliefs?**
   To encourage foreign investments or promote a certain policy.

4. **What happens when a taxpayer pays too much tax?**
   They are entitled to claim a tax refund.

READING 1 KEY VOCABULARY

tax return	tax compliance	tax planning
tax consulting	tax due diligence report	tax authorities
full business name	company registration number	tax identification number
holding company	subsidiary	predominant activity
taxable income	tax base	allowable deductions
gross income	be exempt from paying tax	disadvantaged tax payers
tax credit	tax relief	incentive
tax liability	tax refund	tax rate

4. SPEAKING 1

Students provide answers based on the local circumstances. Encourage a discussion on effectiveness of tax reliefs. Ask what type of tax reliefs they would introduce. Let students speak freely and do not overcorrect.

Tax Accounting

5. FOCUS ON VOCABULARY: Tax Collocations

1.	impose (levy)	A	a tax
2.	attain	B	tax compliance
3.	apply	C	a tax rate to tax base
4.	be subject to	D	taxation
5.	be exempt from	E	paying taxes
6.	employ	F	tax planning strategies
7.	prepare	G	a tax due diligence report
8.	determine	H	taxable income
9.	be entitled to	I	claim tax deductions
10.	minimise	J	tax liability

6. LANGUAGE TASK: Collocations Applied

Students create their own sentences, based on their own professional experience.

7. FOCUS ON GRAMMAR: Going to + Infinitive for Future Predictions

The first part of the exercise is designed to facilitate a controlled practice, while the second part provides an opportunity for a freer discussion.

8. READING 2: Introduction

Start with the general classification of taxes (direct and indirect) and then move to individual forms of taxes. Ask students to tell you about all forms of taxation they know, in any order.

1. How can taxes be generally classified?
   Generally, taxes are divided into two groups: direct and indirect taxes.

2. What is the difference between direct and indirect taxes?
   Direct taxes are imposed on income, property, etc. of individuals or companies, whereas indirect taxes are levied on goods or services.

3. How can the burden of indirect taxes be shifted from one taxpayer to another?
   By an increase of price of goods and services.

4. What tax do physical persons pay on their income?
   Personal Income Tax.

5. What tax do companies pay on their net income?
   Corporation Tax (US: Corporate Income Tax)

6. What tax do companies pay on capital gains?
   Capital Gains Tax.

7. What is capital gain?
   Income earned through disposal of asset other than inventory.

8. What tax is imposed on consumption of goods and services?
   Value Added Tax (VAT).
   Note: Sales Tax is still in use in the USA.

9. What type of tax do real estate owners pay?
   Property Tax.

10. What government authority usually imposes property tax?
    The local government.

11. How is the amount of property tax determined?
    It is based on the estimated value of property.

12. What tax is levied on purchase of houses, flats, land and buildings?
    Stamp Duty Land Tax (US: Transfer Tax)

13. What tax is imposed on individuals who inherit assets from a deceased person?
    Inheritance Tax.

14. What indirect tax is levied on specific products with a view to discouraging their consumption?
    Excise Duty.

15. What tax is charged on merchandise imported from one country to another?
    Customs Duty.

16. Why do local governments (municipalities) impose taxes?
    To fund local government services.

9. READING COMPREHENSION 2: Answers

1. **What is the difference between direct and indirect taxes?**
   Direct taxes are imposed on income, property, wealth of individuals or companies. They are paid directly to government. Indirect taxes are levied on goods and services and paid by consumers.

2. **What tax do companies pay on their income?**
   Corporation Tax (US: Corporate Income Tax).

3. **What tax is imposed at different stages of production?**
   VAT.

4. **What are the reasons for imposing excise duty?**
   Discouraging consumption of the good that is being taxed. In addition, excise duties usually represent a significant source of state income.

Tax Accounting

READING 2 KEY VOCABULARY

direct tax	indirect tax	to levy a tax	income tax
corporation tax	capital gains tax	VAT	to impose a tax
property tax	stamp duty land tax	inheritance tax	customs duty
excise duty	to charge a tax	to discourage consumption	pollution tax

10. SPEAKING 2

Let students speak freely and do not overcorrect.

11. WRITING TASK

Assign the writing task for homework.

12. BUILDING UP A NEW VOCABULARY

1.	tax return	A	a standard form provided by tax authorities on which a taxpayer reports taxable income
2.	taxable income	B	an income that is subject to taxation after all deductions
3.	tax deduction	C	a deduction from gross income that arises due to various types of expenses incurred by a taxpayer
4.	tax allowance	D	a part of income which a person is allowed to earn and not pay tax on
5.	tax credit	E	a tax incentive which allows certain taxpayers to subtract the amount from the amount of tax owed
6.	tax refund	F	a return of excess amounts of tax, when the tax liability is less than the taxes paid
7.	tax relief	G	any programme or incentive that reduces the amount of tax owed
8.	tax liability	H	the total amount of tax that an entity or individual is legally obligated to pay
9.	corporate income tax (UK: corporation tax)	I	a direct tax levied by the government on profits of a company
10.	personal income tax	J	a direct tax imposed by the government on a person's annual income

UNIT 9

UNIT MAP

Reading 1	Accounting Department
Reading 2	Cash Collection, Cash Disbursement and Procurement
Focus on Vocabulary	Procurement Terms
Language Task	Describing Purchasing Goods Process
Focus on Grammar	Present Continuous for Future Arrangements
Writing Task	Payroll Tax Report
Extra Activity 1	Completing an Invoice *(see page 113)*
Extra Activity 2	Collecting Overdue Accounts *(see Student's Book, page 125)*

1. INTRODUCTION TO THE UNIT

> Unit 9 examines different functions of a company's accounting department. The first part of the Unit focuses on payroll, calculation of payroll taxes and social security contributions.
>
> The second part of the Unit analyses other tasks administered by the accounting department: cash collection, cash disbursement and procurement. The aim of this section is to provide a natural context for the use of relevant vocabulary, rather than analysing the accounting procedures in detail.

2. READING 1: Introduction

Ask students to name different tasks performed by the accounting department. Lead the conversation towards payroll, cash collection, cash disbursement and procurement.

1. What functions does the accounting department in your company perform?
2. In addition to maintaining financial records, what other functions does a company's accounting department perform?
   It administers payroll, cash collection, cash disbursement and procurement.
3. What does the term payroll refer to?
   The term payroll has several meanings and it may refer to: **a)** *a financial record of employee's salaries and wages;* **b)** *a list of employees receiving wages or salaries;* **c)** *the total sum of money to be paid out to employees at a given time;*
4. What is the difference between salary and wage?
   Salary is a fixed amount of payment, whereas wage is based on the number of hours worked.
5. How do accountants calculate payroll?
   They calculate gross earnings and make deductions. In addition, they calculate overtime, sick pay, holidays and bonuses.
6. What are typical deductions against gross earnings?
   Income tax and social security contributions.
7. What do social security contributions include?
   They generally include health, pension and unemployment insurance.
8. What do payroll taxes consist of?
   Taxes paid by an employee and taxes paid by an employer.
9. How are taxes paid by an employee collected?
   They are withheld by an employer from employees' salaries and wages and paid directly to the government.
10. In addition to salary, what other forms of remuneration are available to employees?
    Bonuses, commissions, employee benefits, sick pay, maternity leave payment, etc.
11. Is withholding tax levied only on salaries and wages?
    Generally, it is applied to all forms of remuneration.
12. How do employees find out about the amount of taxes and contributions paid?
    Through a payslip (US pay stub).

3. READING COMPREHENSION 1: Answers

1. **How do accountants calculate payroll?**
   They first calculate gross earnings for both hourly and salaried employees and then make deductions. In addition, they calculate overtime, sick pay, holidays and bonuses.

2. **What do deductions against gross earnings include?**
   Income tax and social security contributions.

3. **What do social security contributions generally consist of?**
   Health, pension and unemployment insurance.

4. **How are payroll taxes paid by an employee collected?**
   They are withheld by an employer from employees' salaries or wages and paid directly to tax authorities.

READING 1 KEY VOCABULARY

payroll	cash collection	cash disbursement
remuneration	procurement	gross earnings
deductions	employee benefits	overtime
sick pay	income tax	maternity leave
health insurance	pension insurance	unemployment insurance
payslip	social security contribution	payroll tax
withholding tax		

4. SPEAKING 1

Students provide answers based on the local circumstances.

5. FOCUS ON VOCABULARY

Although the procurement process is analysed in Reading 2, this exercise introduces the main procurement-
-related terms beforehand. Before doing the exercise, ask students to reconstruct the process of procuring goods in their own companies. Introduce and explain new words if necessary: *purchase requisition form; quotation; suppliers' bids; purchase order; supplier's invoice.*

1. Prepare purchase requisition
2. Check and authorise requisition
3. Send out requests for quotations
4. Compare supplier bids
5. Select a supplier
6. Issue a purchase order
7. Receive and inspect goods (AE)
8. Accept or reject goods
9. Receive a delivery note and invoice (AE)
10. Reconcile the invoice and the purchase order
11. Post the supplier's invoice (AE)
12. Prepare and authorise payment
13. Pay the supplier's invoice (AE)
14. Enter payment into payment records (AE)

An accounting entry is made at steps 7, 9, 11, 12, 13, 14.

6. LANGUAGE TASK: Describing Purchasing Goods Process

Students describe the procurement process as it takes place in their companies, using the vocabulary from the previous exercise. The exercise could be done in pairs, with students comparing their company's practices.

7. FOCUS ON GRAMMAR

To emphasise the future arrangement concept, ask students whether they use a personal organiser (diary, etc.). Before doing the exercise, you might ask students about their scheduled appointments for this week, month, etc. This is also a good opportunity for introducing the vocabulary related to arranging a suitable time, acceptance, polite refusals, etc.

Example: *Does five o'clock on Monday suit you? Five o'clock suits me perfectly. / I'm afraid I have prior engagements.*

8. Reading 2: Introduction

The second part of the Unit examines other tasks administered by the accounting department. New vocabulary should be introduced and explained at this stage: *terms of payment; date of maturity; outstanding invoice; overdue invoice; delinquent accounts, default; enforced collection; etc.*

1. What accounting term refers to money owed to a company by its debtors?
   Accounts receivable.
2. Who is responsible for recovery of cash from accounts receivable?
   Cash Collection Department / Officer.
3. Which financial statement reports information on accounts receivable?
   They are reported as current assets on a company's balance sheet, assuming they are due within one fiscal year.
4. What is the primary objective of cash collection department?
   To collect all unpaid invoices before they become overdue.
5. What document identifies a transaction between a buyer and seller?
   Invoice.
6. What do 'terms of payment' stated on an invoice define?
   Terms of payment define the time in which payment must be made and how it must be made.
7. What does the term 'date of maturity' refer to?
   It refers to the date when an invoice must be paid.
8. What does the term 'outstanding invoice' refer to?
   It refers to an unpaid invoice not yet due.
9. What does the term 'overdue invoice' refer to?
   It refers to a past due invoice.
10. What are 'delinquent accounts'?
    Past due accounts.
11. When does delinquency usually occur?
    It usually occurs before a default is declared.
12. What is 'default in payment'?
    It is a situation when a debtor is unable to pay a debt.
13. What might a company that issued the invoice do in that situation?
    It may decide to take a legal action against the debtor to enforce collection of delinquent accounts.
14. What does the term 'cash disbursement' refer to?
    It refers to payment of money to settle obligations to accounts payable, meet a company's operating expenses or pay interests for loans.
15. In what forms can cash disbursement be made?
    It can be made in form of cash, plastic money, cheques or electronic fund transfers.

16. What accounting term means 'money owed to suppliers'?
    Accounts payable.

17. Which financial statement reports information on accounts payable?
    They are reported as current liabilities on a company's balance sheet, as they are expected to be fulfilled within one year.

18. What does the term 'reconciliation of bank accounts' refer to?
    It refers to comparison of a company's bank accounts with its general ledger accounts.

19. What are the responsibilities of the procurement department?
    Keeping track of purchase orders, keeping record of all liabilities that arise from purchases on credit, keeping track of a company's inventory, performing inventory counts.

20. What is a purchase order?
    A document sent to vendor by the purchasing department, ordering a purchase.

21. In large companies, what precedes issuing a purchase order?
    In large companies purchase order is issued after an internal request to procure goods.

22. What is the name of the document that initiates a purchase of merchandise?
    Purchase requisition.

23. What does the term inventory refer to?
    It refers to goods held for sale.

9. READING COMPREHENSION 2: Answers

1. **What does the term cash collection refer to?**
   It refers to recovery of cash from accounts receivable.

2. **What is the difference between outstanding and overdue invoices?**
   An outstanding invoice is an unpaid invoice not yet due, whereas an overdue invoice is a past due invoice.

3. **What does the term 'cash disbursement' refer to?**
   It refers to payment of money to settle obligations to accounts payable, meet a company's operating expenses or pay interests for loans.

4. **What is reconciliation of bank accounts?**
   Comparison of a company's bank accounts with its general ledger accounts.

Unit 9

READING 2 KEY VOCABULARY

accounts receivable	trade debtors	cash collection cycle
invoice	overdue	terms of payment
credit terms	date of maturity	delinquent accounts
default	enforced collection	to settle obligations
electronic fund transfer	reconciliation of bank account	vendor
purchase order	purchase requisition form	

10. SPEAKING 2

Let students speak freely and do not overcorrect.

11. WRITING TASK

Assign the writing task for homework.

12. BUILDING UP A NEW VOCABULARY

1. Payroll	A	a list of employees receiving wages or salaries, with the amounts due to each
2. Cash Disbursement	B	payments made by a company during a specified period
3. Purchase Order	C	a written authorisation from a buyer to acquire goods or services
4. Procurement	D	the act of obtaining or buying goods and service
5. Sick Pay	E	money given by an employer to someone who cannot work because of illness
6. Social Security Contributions	F	compulsory payments paid to the government to receive a future social benefit
7. Payroll Tax	G	a tax that an employer withholds and/or pays on behalf of their employees based on the wage or salary of the employee
8. Withholding Tax	H	income tax withheld from employees' wages and paid directly to the government by the employee
9. Outstanding Invoice	I	an unpaid invoice not yet due
10. Overdue Invoice	J	an invoice not paid at a required time

UNIT 10

UNIT MAP

Reading 1	IFRS
Reading 2	Fundamental Accounting Principles
Focus on Vocabulary	Global Financial Reporting Language
Language Task	IFRS Adoption: Pro et Contra
Focus on Grammar	Passive Voice
Writing Task	Application of Accounting Principles in Professional Practice
Extra Activity 1	Accounting Principles in Professional Practice 1 *(see page 114)*

1. INTRODUCTION TO THE UNIT

> The first part of Unit 1 focuses on International Financial Reporting Standards, a set of common rules and principles that guide the standardised international financial reporting. The Unit examines the reasons why they were created, their objectives, their importance and advantages and disadvantages of their adoption.
>
> The second part of Unit 2 examines some of the fundamental accounting principles and reveals how they guide the preparation of financial statements.

2. READING 1: Introduction

You can start the class by having a general discussion on the global mobility of capital, leading it to the need for standardised financial reporting. Ask students to explain the meaning of the phrase *'Today, the world's financial markets are borderless'*.

Possible answers: Companies seek capital at the best price wherever it is available. Investors and lenders seek investment opportunities wherever they can get the best returns corresponding to the risks involved.

1. What do investors need in order to assess the risks of investment opportunities worldwide?
   They need financial information that is comparable across borders.

2. What rules and guidelines must accountants follow when reporting financial data?
   Accounting principles.

3. What document outlines internationally accepted accounting principles?
   International Financial Reporting Standards.

4. What are International Financial Reporting Standards?
   A set of accounting standards stating how particular types of transactions and other events should be reported in financial statements.

5. What are the benefits of standardised recording and reporting of business transactions?
   It ensures consistency, transparency and comparability of financial reporting in the global economy.

6. What is the primary objective of these standards?
   To identify risks hidden in various sections of financial statements and make them clearly visible.

7. How do the standards help investors?
   They make it easier for investors and other stakeholders to get a clear picture of the company they are considering for investment.

8. How widespread is the adoption of IFRS around the world?
   Currently, about 120 countries require IFRS for domestic listed companies (2019).

9. What are the advantages of IFRS adoption?
   By adopting IFRS, a company can present its financial statements on the same basis as its foreign competitors, making comparison easier. Furthermore, companies with subsidiaries in countries that require or permit IFRS may be able to use one accounting system company-wide.

10. What are the disadvantages of IFRS adoption?
    It requires high costs. Small companies might not have sufficient resources to implement the changes, train staff or hire accountants. In addition, some countries might not be willing to surrender the standard-setting authority to an international body.

11. What are the economic consequences of IFRS adoption?
    Possible answers: *Supposedly, it increases the level of a foreign investment flow. In addition, it facilities an easier trade with the countries that have already adopted IFRS. On the other hand, it might bring increased costs for small and medium enterprises, which are subject to IFRS adoption.*

3. READING COMPREHENSION 1: Answers

1. **What regulatory body issues IFRS?**
   International Accounting Standards Board

2. **What is the primary objective of IFRS?**
   To identify risks hidden in various sections of financial statements and make them clearly visible to allow making an effective comparison.

3. **How does it help investors?**
   It makes it easier for investors and other stakeholders to get a clear picture of the company they are considering for investment.

4. **Why is adoption of IFRS important?**
   For several reasons: it simplifies investment decisions as investors can compare financial statements, regardless of the company's country of origin; ensures that companies adopt similar fundamental rules in reporting their activities; improves transparency.

Unit 10

READING 1 KEY VOCABULARY

guidelines	to adhere to	accounting principles
underlying concept	regulatory body	standardised reporting
consistency	transparency	comparability
stakeholder	IFRS adoption	conceptual framework

4. SPEAKING 1

Students provide answers based on the local circumstances and their personal experience.

5. FOCUS ON VOCABULARY

Introduce the collocations first, as they provide the key to the second part of the exercise. Explain beforehand any new words if necessary. Ask students to work in groups and expand collocations into sentences.

1. IFRS are a critical source of information published annually, useful to various **stakeholders** (shareholders, debtors, clients, employees and governments).

2. Adoption of IFRS is essential for attaining **transparency**, **accountability** and **consistency** in global financial reporting.

3. The use of a single set of financial reporting standards across countries has increased the **comparability** of financial statements across borders.

4. Some people view IASB as a **regulatory body** that privileges commercial interests.

5. IFRS **outline** the basis for accounting and reporting in companies.

6. This position involves reviewing and ensuring **adherence** to IFRS and statutory accounting policies.

7. The IFRS **conceptual framework** describes the concepts that underlie the preparation and presentation of financial statements.

8. Accrual accounting is one of the **underlying concepts** of IFRS.

6. LANGUAGE TASK

Let students discuss freely and do not overcorrect. Some of the arguments in favour and against the adoption have been presented in the Introduction to Reading 1.

Guiding Principles of Accounting

7. FOCUS ON GRAMMAR

The first activity is a simple controlled practice, which can be used to review passive voice with different tenses if necessary (*What activities were performed in your office last week? What activities will be performed in your office next month?*). You can vary and personalise the exercise by asking students to describe the phases of a specific accounting or audit engagement, or any other procedures regularly carried out in their business organisation. The second activity gives students more freedom to create their own sentences.

8. READING 2: Introduction

Ask students to name some of the key accounting principles and explain what they prescribe. In a stronger class, you may distribute cut outs and ask students to explain the concept without naming the actual principle.

Business Entity Principle

1. Into what two groups are business entities generally classified?
   Incorporated and unincorporated entities.

2. What is the main characteristic of incorporated business entities?
   They are separate legal entities from their owners.

3. What does the business entity concept state?
   It states that that the activity of a business is separate from the personal activities of the owner(s) and employees.

Conservatism

4. What does the conservatism principle mean for accountants?
   This principle states that given two options in valuation of business transactions, the amount recorded should be the lower rather than the higher value.

5. How does this principle help accountants?
   It helps them decide between two alternatives.

6. Does this principle allow accountants to anticipate both losses and gains?
   No, it only allows accountants to anticipate losses.

7. What are the examples of conservatism principle?
   Possible answer: *Making provisions for doubtful debts.*

Objectivity (Reliability) Principle

8. What does the objectivity principle state?
   The objectivity principle states that accountants should only record those transactions for which they can obtain objective evidence. In addition, it states that bookkeeping and financial recording should be performed with independence, that is, free of bias and prejudice.

9. What is the objective evidence for recording transactions?
   A document such as purchase receipt, bank statement, supplier invoice, etc.

Relevance Principle

10. What does the term relevance mean in accounting?
    In accounting the term relevance means it will make a difference to a decision maker.

11. What does the relevance principle state?
    The relevance principle states that financial information, in order to be useful to external users, must be relevant.

Matching Principle

12. What does the matching principle state?
    The matching principle states that, when measuring net income for an accounting period, the expenses incurred in that period should be matched against the revenue generated in the same period.

Going Concern Principle

13. What does the term 'going concern' mean in accounting?
    It is an assumption that the entity will remain in business for the foreseeable future. In other words, a company will continue its operation without threat of liquidation within a reasonably short period.

14. What indicators show that the entity possibly faces going concern problems?
    Possible answers: A significant decrease of sales revenues; a large amount of debt or interest payable overdue; a large overdraft; loss of key management; lack of funds invested in R&D; cash flow problems.

Full Disclosure Principle

15. What does the full disclosure principle state?
    It states that financial statements of an entity should include all information that would affect a reader's understanding of those statements.

16. How do accountants decide what information to disclose?
    They disclose only information about events that are likely to have a material impact on the entity's financial position or results.

9. READING COMPREHENSION 2: Answers

1. **What aspect of incorporated entities is of the key relevance for the business entity principle?**
   The fact that that incorporated business entities are separate legal entities from their owners.

2. **What does the application of conservatism principle ensure?**
   It ensures that assets and income are not overstated and liabilities and expenses are not understated.

3. **What does the term relevance mean in accounting? Illustrate with examples from your professional practice.**
   In accounting, the term relevance means it will make a difference to a decision maker.

4. **What assumption is the basis of the going concern principle?**
   The assumption that an entity will remain in business for the foreseeable future.

Guiding Principles of Accounting

READING 2 KEY VOCABULARY

business entity principle	incorporated entity	legal entity
conservatism principle	to anticipate	to overstate
to understate	objectivity principle	unbiased
relevance principle	matching principle	to offset
going concern principle	assumption	liquidation
foreseeable future	full disclosure principle	

10. SPEAKING 2

Students provide answers based on their professional practice.

11. WRITING TASK

Assign the writing task for homework.

12. BUILDING UP A NEW VOCABULARY

1.	consistency	A	the quality of something that follows the same pattern and does not vary in quality
2.	transparency	B	visibility or accessibility of information, especially concerning business practices
3.	comparability	C	the quality of being comparable, capable of being compared
4.	stakeholder	D	a person with an interest or concern in something, especially a business
5.	incorporated	E	formed as a legal corporation
6.	legal entity	F	any business organisation that is legally permitted to enter into a contract
7.	to anticipate	G	to expect something to occur, to foresee
8.	to overstate	H	to say that something is larger or greater than it really is
9.	to understate	I	to say that something is smaller than it really is
10.	unbiased	J	impartial, free from all prejudice and favouritism

UNIT 11

UNIT MAP

Reading 1	Corporate Crimes
Reading 2	Internal Control
Focus on Vocabulary	Types of Corporate Crimes
Language Task	Describing Corporate Crimes
Focus on Grammar	First Conditional
Writing Task	Report on Internal Control Measures
Extra Activity 1	Real Life Crimes *(see page 115)*
Extra Activity 2	Accounting Frauds *(see page 116)*
Extra Activity 3	Internal Control Measures *(see page 117)*

1. INTRODUCTION TO THE UNIT

The first part of Unit 11 begins by presenting various types of corporate crimes, leading to accounting fraud, embezzlement and tax evasion, the key accounting related white-collar crimes. The total list of corporate crimes is quite extensive and the teacher should decide on the scope of the vocabulary being introduced.

The second part of the Unit introduces the concept of internal control and what it means in accounting. The Unit analyses the aims of internal control, internal control measures and its importance for external and internal audit.

2. READING 1: Introduction

You may start the class by asking students to interpret the phrase *'with creative accounting who needs cheating'*. This should steer the discussion towards the difference between the accounting fraud and creative accounting, and the thin line between the two.

1. What does the term 'corporate crime' refer to?
   Corporate crime is a crime committed by a corporation or business entity or by individuals who are acting on behalf of a corporation or business entity.

2. Who are typical perpetrators of corporate crimes?
   Business executives, accountants, financial advisers, business owners, etc.

3. What are the typical penalties for corporate crimes?
   Fines or prison sentences, depending on the gravity of the crime.

4. How do state authorities combat corporate crimes in your country?
   Possible answers: *Through the criminal justice system, regulatory agencies and legislation.*

5. What are the most common types of corporate crimes?
   Accounting fraud; tax fraud; tax evasion; embezzlement; (Other white-collar crimes: falsification of records; forgery of signatures; inventory fraud; bribery; short-shipment; sales skimming; pilfering; money laundering; insider trading; industrial espionage; bid rigging; etc.)

6. Ask students to explain what accounting fraud is.
   Intentional misrepresentation or manipulation of accounting records.

7. What is the aim of accounting fraud?
   Possible answer: *To make a company's financial performance seem better than it actually is, with a view to increasing the share price.*

8. What forms may accounting fraud take?
   Possible answers: *Manipulating sales and accounts receivables, manipulating stock, understating liabilities and expense, overstating assets, etc.*

9. Ask students to provide examples of accounting fraud they know.

10. What is creative accounting?
    The exploitation of loopholes in financial regulations in order to gain advantage or present figures in a misleadingly favourable light.

11. A dishonest financial adviser misappropriates funds entrusted to him. What type of white collar crime is that?
    Embezzlement.

12. Ask students to provide examples of embezzlement they know.

13. Ask students to explain what tax fraud is.
    A general term that describes any illegal intentional attempt to evade tax laws.

14. Ask students to explain what tax evasion is.
    A type of tax fraud referring to an illegal non-payment or underpayment of tax liability.
15. What is the aim of tax evasion?
    To hide profit.
16. What forms may tax evasion take?
    It can range from simply filing tax forms with false information to illegally transferring property in order to avoid tax obligations.
17. What is tax avoidance?
    The minimisation of tax liability by lawful methods.
18. Ask students to talk about tax evasion and tax avoidance methods used by large companies with subsidiaries abroad. Steer the discussion towards transfer pricing issues.
19. How is transfer pricing related to tax evasion and tax avoidance?
    Tax evasion is performed through transfer pricing. Companies minimise taxes and increase profits by ensuring that most profits are located in low tax jurisdictions.
20. What is transfer pricing?
    Setting the price for goods and services sold between related entities within an enterprise.
21. What principle determines the setting of a fair price among related entities?
    The arm's length principle.
22. What might be an additional motive for tax evasion?
    To hide funds obtained through illegal activities, i.e. to avoid money laundering charges.

Additional Vocabulary
If relevant, introduce the corporate crimes listed below:

falsification: changing figures, records, etc. so that they contain false information
forgery: copying something, a signature for instance, in order to deceive people
inventory fraud: inventory (warehousing) frauds involve misappropriating inventory for personal use, stealing inventory and scrap for sale to outsiders, etc.
bribery: offering money to someone in return for a favour
short-shipment: short-shipment occurs when cargo received is less than what is stipulated by documents on hand
sales skimming: employees who skim from their companies steal sales or receivables before they are recorded in the company books
pilfering: pilfering refers to stealing things that are not worth much, especially from the place of work
money laundering: the process of making illegally-gained proceeds appear legal
insider trading: the illegal practice of trading on the stock exchange to one's own advantage through having access to confidential information
industrial espionage: spying and theft of trade secrets
bid-rigging (collusive tendering): occurs when two or more competitors agree they will not compete genuinely with each other for tenders, allowing one of the members to 'win' the tender

Corporate Crime and Internal Controls

3. READING COMPREHENSION 1: Answers

1. **What is the primary motive for accounting fraud?**
   To make a company's financial performance seem better than it actually is.

2. **What are some of the embezzlement schemes?**
   Stealing cash without making a record of the transaction; staff claiming expenses for items that are not business related; payroll fraud (adding fictitious individuals to a company payroll); fraudulent vendor purchases (creating a fictitious supplier and documentation); improper use of client funds by their investment advisers.

3. **What is transfer pricing?**
   Setting the price for goods and services sold between related entities.

4. **What are the possible motives for tax evasion?**
   Unwillingness to pay taxes or exposure to money laundering charges.

READING 1 KEY VOCABULARY

corporate crime	fraud	embezzlement
bribery	falsification	forgery
short-shipment	misappropriation	insider trading
money laundering	misrepresentation	financial performance
creative accounting	cooking the books	to overstate
to understate	payroll fraud	fraudulent
fictitious	underpayment	transfer pricing
arm's length principle	related entities	money laundering

4. SPEAKING 1

Students provide answers based on their opinions.

5. FOCUS ON VOCABULARY: Types of Corporate Crimes

1. **Fraud** is an intentional use of deceit, a trick or some other dishonest means to deprive someone of their money, property of legal rights.
2. **Tax Fraud** is a general term that describes various violations of tax laws.
3. **Tax Evasion** refers to use of illegal methods to avoid paying tax.
4. **Embezzlement** is stealing money from one's employer.
5. **Insider Trading:** the illegal practice of trading on the stock exchange to one's own advantage through having access to confidential information.
6. **Bribery** means offering money to someone in return for a favour.
7. **Falsification** refers to changing figures, records, etc., so that they contain false information.
8. **Forgery (Counterfeiting)** means copying something, a signature for instance, in order to deceive people.
9. **Short-Shipment** occurs when cargo received is less than what is stipulated by documents on hand.
10. **Pilfering** refers to stealing things that are not worth much, especially from the place of work.
11. **Industrial Espionage** means spying and theft of trade secrets.
12. **Front Company** is a subsidiary used to conceal illegal activities.

6. LANGUAGE TASK

Students describe corporate crimes they have heard of.

7. FOCUS ON GRAMMAR

The aim of the exercise is to review the use of first conditional in a realistic context. Go through the vocabulary first, if necessary.

8. READING 2: Introduction

You may start the class by asking students what measures management takes in order to prevent corporate crimes from occurring in the first place. The discussion should be steered towards internal control, types of internal control activities and their purpose. The internal control related vocabulary is quite complex and its scope should be adjusted to the abilities of your class.

1. What does the term internal control generally refer to?
   In brief, it refers to policies and procedures implemented to ensure the continued reliability of accounting systems. More specifically, it is a process designed to improve effectiveness and efficiency of a company's operations; reliability of financial reporting; compliance with applicable laws; deter error and employee fraud.

2. What are the aims of internal control activities?
   To enable an organisation to conduct its business in an orderly and efficient manner; to safeguard a company's assets and resources; to deter and detect errors, fraud and theft; to ensure accuracy and completeness of accounting data; to produce timely financial and management information;

3. What type of internal control activities do companies perform?
   A wide range of diverse activities such as approvals, authorisations, verifications, reconciliations, performance reviews, security maintenance; preparation and maintenance of related records that provide evidence of execution of these activities.

4. What are the possible limitations of internal control and why do they occur?
   The limitations arise as a result of inadequate segregation of duties; internal control being bypassed by management; employee carelessness; misunderstanding of instructions; errors in judgement;

5. Who is responsible for introducing systems of internal control?
   Board of directors, senior management and executives.

6. Why is internal control important for external auditors?
   External auditors rely on the system of internal controls when giving a favourable opinion to financial statements.

7. Why is internal control important for internal auditors?
   Because internal audit is an essential part of internal control process.

8. Ask students to describe internal control activities their companies perform.

Unit 11

9. READING COMPREHENSION 2: Answers

1. **What does internal control mean in accounting?**

   It is defined as a process aimed at providing reasonable assurance that a company is operating efficiently, financial reporting is reliable and the company is in compliance with applicable laws, regulations and policies.

2. **What is the aim of internal control?**

   To enable an organisation to conduct its business in an orderly and efficient manner, safeguard a company's assets and resources, deter and detect errors, fraud and theft, ensure accuracy and completeness of accounting data and produce timely financial and management information.

3. **What activities does internal control involve?**

   Approvals, authorisations, verifications, reconciliations, performance reviews, security maintenance, as well as preparation and maintenance of related records that provide evidence of execution of these activities.

4. **Why is internal control important for external auditors?**

   They rely on the system of internal controls when giving a favourable opinion to financial statements.

READING 2 KEY VOCABULARY

internal control	stakeholder	assurance
applicable laws	deterrent	to safeguard
approval	authorisation	verification
reconciliation	performance review	security maintenance
internal auditor	external auditor	limitations
segregation of duties	bypassing internal controls	carelessness

10. SPEAKING 2

Students provide answers based on their company's circumstances.

11. WRITING TASK

Assign the writing task for homework.

12. BUILDING UP A NEW VOCABULARY

1.	assurance	A	the state of being sure or certain about something
2.	applicable laws	B	laws in force
3.	deterrent	C	a thing that discourages or is intended to discourage someone from doing something
4.	to safeguard	D	to protect
5.	verification	E	the use of tests to ensure the accuracy or truth of the information
6.	accounting fraud	F	intentional manipulation of financial statements
7.	segregation of duties	G	the concept of having more than one person required to complete a task
8.	accountability	H	the obligation of an individual or organisation to account for its activities, accept responsibility for them
9.	be in compliance	I	be in conformity
10.	embezzlement	J	a type of fraud where a person steals a company's assets

UNIT 12

UNIT MAP

Reading 1	Accrual-Basis Accounting
Reading 2	Timing differences
Focus on Vocabulary	Accrual-Basis Accounting Key Terms
Language Task	Accrual-Basis Method Applied in Practice
Focus on Grammar	Second Conditional
Writing Task	Cash-Basis Vs Accrual-Basis Method
Extra Activity 1	Identify the Timing Difference *(see page 118)*
Extra Activity 2	Ethical Dilemmas *(see Student's Book, page 131)*

1. INTRODUCTION TO THE UNIT

> Unit 12 examines two approaches to recording transactions, the accrual and the cash-basis method. The accrual-basis method is a standard approach for most companies, while the cash-basis method is mainly presented to juxtapose the two and illustrate the reasons for using the accrual-basis method.
>
> The second part of the Unit analyses timing differences, which occur as a result of application of the accrual-basis method. The timing differences concern the difference between the transaction event and the transfer of cash. Each timing difference is analysed individually.

2. READING 1: Introduction

The accrual-basis accounting method states that revenues and expenses are recorded when earned or incurred, not when the cash is paid. This concept can be illustrated by the following examples:

1. A company was paid in January $ 1,000 for the consulting work completed and invoiced in December. When is the transaction recorded?
   In December.

2. A company pays an electricity bill in July for the electricity used in June. When is the transaction recorded?
   In June.

3. What are the two main approaches to recording transactions?
   The cash-basis and the accrual-basis accounting method.

4. What is the difference between the two methods?
   Under the cash-basis method, income is recorded when cash is received and expenses are recorded when cash is paid. Under the accrual-basis method transactions are recorded as they take place in business, not when cash changes hand.

5. What are the disadvantages of the cash-basis accounting?
   It does not always give an accurate picture of a company's performance.

6. Ask students to provide examples that illustrate the above.
   Possible answer: *A company may incur losses related to a business activity in one year, and generate income related to the same activity in the following year. If transactions are recorded using the cash-basis method, financial statements based on this information will be misleading.*

7. Which key accounting principle supports the accrual-basis method of recording transactions?
   The matching principle.

8. What does the matching principle state?
   Under the matching principle, revenues and related expenses are recorded within the same reporting period, (i.e. the matching principle offsets revenue against the related expenses).

9. Why is recording revenues and related expenses within the same reporting period important?
   Because it enables accountants to evaluate effects of business transactions fully, i.e. whether profit is made or losses are incurred.

10. What is the key disadvantage of accrual-basis accounting?
    It does not give a true representation of cash flow, i.e. a company may appear profitable on paper and have no cash in bank.

11. How is this disadvantage overcome?
    By careful monitoring of a company's cash flow.

12. What is the effect of accrual-basis accounting on taxes?
    The downside of this method is that companies pay income taxes on revenue before they actually received it.

Unit 12

3. READING COMPREHENSION 1: Answers

1. **Why might financial statements prepared on cash-basis be misleading?**
   A company may incur losses related to a business activity in one year, and generate income related to the same activity in the following year. Other scenario is that a company receives payment for the business activity in one year, and incurs related expenses in the following year. In both cases, financial statements prepared on cash-basis do not reflect the true financial performance.

2. **At what point are revenues and expenses recorded under the accrual-basis method?**
   Revenues are recorded when they are earned and expenses are recorded when they are incurred.

3. **Which accounting principle does the accrual-basis method support?**
   The matching principle.

4. **What is the main disadvantage of the accrual-basis method?**
   It does not provide an accurate representation of cash flow.

READING 1 KEY VOCABULARY

accrual-basis method	cash-basis method	secure a contract
generate gains	misleading	matching principle
monitoring cash-flow	accurate representations	to evaluate effects

4. SPEAKING 1

Students speculate on possible scenarios. Focus on situations such as the revenue awaiting collection; investment in plant and equipment; cash received used for additional inventory; etc.

5. FOCUS ON VOCABULARY: Key Accrual-Basis Terms

1. Accrual accounting is an accounting method that measures the performance of a business organisation by recognising **economic events** regardless of when **cash transactions** occur.

2. The term **earned** in revenue recognition generally means when a product is delivered or a service is completed.

3. The term **incurred** in expense recognition refers to the situation when a liability is created or when a cost is paid in cash.

4. The **matching principle** states that all expenses must be matched in the same accounting period as the revenues they helped to generate.

5. Accrual basis accounting allows the current cash inflows or outflows to be combined with future **expected cash inflows or outflows** to give a more accurate picture of a company's financial position.

6. When something finance-related **accrues**, it essentially builds up to be paid or received in future period.
7. The term **accrual** refers to any individual entry recording revenue or expense in the absence of a cash transaction.
8. To **defer** means to delay recognition of certain revenues or expenses.
9. A **deferral** of an expense refers to a payment that was made in one period, but it will not be reported as an expense until a later period.
10. **Deferred** revenue occurs when cash has been received but revenue has not been earned.

6. LANGUAGE TASK

Students use the vocabulary from the exercise to illustrate accounting practices used in their companies.

7. FOCUS ON GRAMMAR

If necessary, revise the difference between the First and Second Conditional before doing the exercise. Stress the fact that the choice of structure will depend on how students see the situations. Extra Activity 2 provides an opportunity for additional practice.

8. READING 2: Introduction

Reading 2 deals with instances when the occurrence of transaction does not coincide with the exchange of cash, i.e. timing differences. Each timing difference is analysed individually.

Prepaid Expense (Deferred Expense)
1. Ask students to think of examples of expenses that a company pays in advance.
   Possible answers: *Supplies, rent, prepaid insurance, advertising fees, licence fees; etc.*
2. How is this expense reported on balance sheet?
   It is recorded as an asset.
3. Why does this account need to be adjusted before the preparation of financial statements?
   Because this adjustment recognises that only a portion of that expense expired in the current year.

Unearned Revenue (Deferred Revenue)
4. Ask students to think of examples of revenues received in advance for goods not yet delivered or services not yet performed.
   Possible answers: *Advance payment for goods to be delivered; prepayment that a company receives in advance for the services it provides.*
5. How is deferred revenue reported on the balance sheet?
   It is recorded as a liability.

6. Why does this account need to be updated before the preparation of financial statements?
   Because this adjustment recognises that only the portion of the unearned revenue has been earned by the end of the year.

Accrued Expenses

7. Ask students to think of examples of expenses incurred, but not yet paid.
   Possible answers: *Salaries payable; taxes payable; interest payable; utility expense;*

8. How is this expense reported on balance sheet?
   It is recorded as a liability.

9. Why does this account need to be updated before preparation of financial statements?
   Without the adjustment, the company's financial statements will not be reporting that the company has incurred the expense.

Accrued Revenue

10. Ask students to think of examples of revenue a company has earned, but hasn't yet invoiced the customer for it.
    Possible answers: *Interest earned from loans; a long-term project paid in arrears;*

    Note: accrued revenue is less common in manufacturing business, since invoices are issued as soon as products are delivered. It more often appears in the industries where billing customers is delayed for a certain period until a designated project milestone is reached. Revenue that has been both earned and invoiced, but not received yet is recorded under accounts receivable.

11. How is this revenue recorded on balance sheet?
    It is recorded as an asset.

16. Why does this account need to be updated prior to preparing financial statements?
    This adjustment recognises that the company provided goods or services that have not been billed yet.

9. READING COMPREHENSION 2: Answers

1. **For what reason do timing differences occur?**
   As a result of revenue or expense being recognised before or after cash is exchanged.

2. **What timing differences are recorded as assets on balance sheet?**
   Accrued revenue and deferred expense.

3. **What timing differences are recorded as liabilities on balance sheet?**
   Deferred revenue and accrued expenses.

4. **What are the reasons for making adjusting entries?**
   To make sure that revenue and expenses are recorded in the appropriate time period.

Accrual Basis Accounting

READING 2 KEY VOCABULARY

to coincide with cash transactions	revenue and expense recognition	timing differences
accrued revenue	to invoice goods and services	accrued expense
deferred revenue	unearned revenue	advance payment
deferred expense	to make an adjusting entry	adjustment

10. SPEAKING 2

Alternatively, students may report on companies they have audited or whose accounts they have examined. Let students speak freely and do not overcorrect.

11. WRITING TASK

Assign the writing task for homework.

12. BUILDING UP A NEW VOCABULARY

1.	accrual-basis accounting	A	an accounting method that records revenues and expenses when they are incurred, regardless of when cash is exchanged
2.	cash basis-accounting	B	an accounting method in which income is recorded when cash is received and expenses are recorded when cash is paid out
3.	economic event	C	any business transaction
4.	matching principle	D	a concept that offsets revenues against related expenses
5.	timing differences	E	the periods between the revenue or expense recognition and the cash transaction
6.	accrued revenue	F	an income the company recognises in its accounts before the cash is received
7.	accrued expense	G	an expense the company recognises in its accounts before it is paid
8.	deferred revenue	H	an income the company recognises in its accounts after the cash is received
9.	deferred expense	I	an expense the company recognises in its accounts after it is paid
10.	advance payment	J	a type of payment that is made ahead of its normal schedule, recorded as prepaid expense in accrual accounting

UNIT 13

UNIT MAP

Reading 1	Depreciation Key Facts
Reading 2	Calculating Depreciation
Focus on Vocabulary	Depreciation Key Terms
Language Task	Depreciating Fixed Assets
Focus on Grammar	Modals of Obligation
Writing Task	Reporting on Depreciation of Fixed Assets
Extra Activity 1	Calculating Depreciation *(see page 119)*
Extra Activity 2	Depreciation Causes *(see page 119)*

1. INTRODUCTION TO THE UNIT

> Unit 13 examines the concept of depreciation as seen from the accounting perspective, which differs from the general concept. The first part of the Unit focuses on different causes of depreciation and how it is recorded in financial statements. This involves an extensive vocabulary content, including terms such as *useful life, residual value, derecognition, wear and tear, obsolescence, accumulated depreciation, historical cost*, etc.
>
> The second part of the Unit analyses the methods for calculating depreciation, along with impairment, another concept related to decline in value of assets. Depending on the ability of the class, the teacher should decide on how extensively these topics should be explored.

2. READING 1: Introduction

Start the lesson by revising what fixed assets are and gradually move to depreciation-related issues.

1. What are fixed assets?
   Assets that are purchased for long-term use and are not likely to be converted quickly into cash, such as land, buildings and equipment.

2. Why do company acquire fixed assets?
   They are intended for regular use and not for resale.

3. Can fixed assets render services indefinitely?
   No. Except for land, all fixed assets have a limited useful life.

4. What is useful life?
   The length of time an asset is expected to be usable for the purpose it was acquired.

5. Is the useful life of an asset the same as its physical life?
   No. Physical life is the length of time an asset would last. Useful life is the period during which an asset is expected to generate revenue.

6. What terms describes the estimated value of an asset at the end of its useful life?
   Salvage value (residual value, scrap value.)

7. What does the book value of a fully depreciated asset equal to?
   It equals to its salvage value.

8. How often should the useful life and the residual value of an asset be reviewed?
   At least at each financial year-end.

9. When does the derecognition of an asset occur?
   On its disposal or when it is withdrawn from use and no future economic benefits are expected.

   Note: derecognition refers to a removal of an item from the balance sheet

10. What costs do companies incur to derive benefit from a fixed asset throughout its useful life?
    Service and maintenance.

11. How are these costs reported on the income statement?
    They are reported as depreciation expense.

12. What is depreciation in general terms?
    A reduction in the value of an asset with the passage of time, due to wear and tear.

13. What does depreciation in accounting context refer to?
    It refers to allocation of cost of assets to periods in which the assets are used.

14. Which accounting principle requires recording of depreciation?
    The matching principle, according to which expenses should be recorded when they occur.

15. What are the causes of depreciation?
    Wear and tear, deterioration, obsolescence, changed market conditions, damages done to the asset, depletion of natural resources (mines, oil fields, quarries, etc.).

16. What is wear and tear?
    Gradual physical deterioration of an asset from age and use.

17. What is obsolescence?
    A loss in value due to development of improved or superior equipment, but not due to physical deterioration.

18. What are the examples of depreciation caused by obsolescence?
    There are numerous possible answers, the most common being depreciation of IT equipment.

19. How is depreciation recorded?
    It is recorded in two accounts: depreciation expense and accumulated depreciation.

20. What is depreciation expense?
    The allocated portion of the cost of a company's fixed assets.

21. In what financial statement is the depreciation expense recorded?
    The depreciation expense account appears on the income statement.

22. What is accumulated depreciation?
    It is the total amount of an asset's cost that has been allocated to depreciation expense since the asset was put into service.

23. In what financial statement is the accumulated depreciation recorded?
    The accumulated depreciation account appears on the balance sheet.

24. What factors are considered when calculating the amount of depreciation expense?
    Historical cost, useful life and salvage value of an asset.

25. What is historical cost?
    The original cost of an asset when acquired by the company.

26. What is depreciable amount?
    It is the difference between the historical cost of an asset and its residual value.

27. What is depreciation rate?
    It is the per cent rate at which an asset is depreciated.

28. What is the tax impact of calculating depreciation?
    For tax purposes, depreciation is an income tax deduction recorded as an expense on a tax return.

3. READING COMPREHENSION 1: Answers

1. **What does the book value of a fully depreciated asset equal to?**
   It equals to its salvage value.

2. **What factors cause depreciation?**
   Wear and tear, deterioration, obsolescence, damage done to the asset or changed market conditions;

3. **Why does obsolescence occur?**
   As a result of new technology, inventions or innovations.

4. **In what accounts is depreciation recorded?**
   Depreciation Expense Account and Accumulated Depreciation Account.

READING 1 KEY VOCABULARY

fixed assets	useful life	salvage value
book value	allocation of costs	depreciation
amortisation	physical deterioration	depletion of natural resources
wear and tear	mishandling	obsolescence
derecognition	depreciation expense	accumulated depreciation

Depreciation

4. SPEAKING 1

Students' answers should be focusing on the fact that tax depreciation is an income tax deduction. On the other hand, the purpose of depreciation in financial accounting is to match the cost of an asset to the revenues earned from using the asset.

5. FOCUS ON VOCABULARY: Depreciation Key Term

1. **Carrying Value of an Asset** is the value of an asset as recorded on the balance sheet, less the accumulated depreciation.
2. **Wear and Tear** is a gradual physical deterioration of an asset that inevitably occurs as a result of normal use or aging.
3. **Useful Life** is the length of time an asset can be productively used in operations.
4. **Physical Deterioration** is a reduction in a property's value resulting from a decline in physical condition.
5. **Accumulated Depreciation** is the total amount of an asset's cost that has been allocated to depreciation expense since the asset was put into service.
6. **Amortisation** refers to spreading an intangible asset's cost over that asset's useful life
7. **Salvage Value** is the projected value that an asset will realise on its sale at the end of its useful life.
8. **Impairment** is a reduction in the recoverable amount of a fixed asset or goodwill below its carrying amount.
9. **Obsolescence** is the process of becoming out-dated or no longer economically feasible, often caused by technology advances.
10. **Historical Cost** is the original cost incurred to acquire an asset.

6. LANGUAGE TASK

The exercise provides students with the opportunity to apply the depreciation vocabulary, as well as to compare the procedures for recording depreciation applied in their companies.

7. FOCUS ON GRAMMAR

The first part of the exercise is designed to provide the context for the revision of modal verbs of obligation, combined with the vocabulary on personal qualities. The second part of the exercise shifts the focus to the past tense of the modals.

8. READING 2: Introduction

1. How is depreciation calculated?
   The residual value is subtracted from the original cost (historical cost) of an asset to determine the net value after the years of use. The net value is then divided by the years the asset was used to arrive at the annual depreciation expense.

2. What are two most common methods of calculating depreciation?
   The straight-line method and the accelerated method.

3. How is depreciation calculated under the straight line method?
   The amount of depreciation does not change over the useful life of an asset, i.e. the same depreciation is calculated over its entire useful life.

4. How is depreciation calculated under the accelerated method?
   The amount of depreciation charged each year is higher during earlier years of an asset's life.

5. What happens when an asset can no longer be converted into cash or provide further use to a business, or has no market value?
   The asset is removed from the balance sheet, i.e. the asset is written off.

6. What happens when a sudden change in circumstances causes the value of an asset to decrease below its book value?
   Impairment is recorded.

7. What is impairment?
   A permanent decline in the value of an asset, which occurs when an asset loses its value to that extent that its fair value is less than its book value.

8. What is a fair value?
   The market value of an asset.

9. How do accountants determine whether an asset is impaired?
   By performing the impairment test, that is, comparing the carrying value (the book value) of a fixed asset to its recoverable amount.

10. What is the impairment loss?
    The amount by which the carrying amount of an asset exceeds its recoverable amount.

11. What might be the causes of impairment?
    Poor management, new competition, technological innovations, obsolescence, etc.

12. Which financial statement reports impairment losses?
    Income statement.

13. What is the difference between depreciation and impairment?
    Impairment is an unplanned decline in the value of assets.

14. How do accountants keep track of how assets depreciate over time?
    They create depreciation schedules.

9. READING COMPREHENSION 2: Answers

1. **How is depreciation calculated under the straight line method?**
   The amount of depreciation does not change over the useful life of an asset, i.e. the same depreciation is calculated over the entire useful life of an asset.

2. **What is the advantage of accelerated depreciation method?**
   It allows faster write-offs.

3. **When does a write-off occur?**
   When an asset can no longer be converted into cash or provide further use to a business.

4. **When does impairment occur?**
   When the fair value of an asset drops below its originally recorded cost.

READING 2 KEY VOCABULARY

straight-line method	accelerated method	write-off
impairment	decline in value	fair value
impairment loss	depreciation schedule	expense charged

10. SPEAKING 2

The discussion should focus on the fact that accelerated depreciation generates higher depreciation expense immediately, and therefore lowers tax payments in the early years of the asset's life.

11. WRITING TASK

Assign the writing task for homework.

12. BUILDING UP A NEW VOCABULARY

1.	to depreciate	A	to lose value over a period of time
2.	to allocate	B	to assign
3.	to deteriorate	C	to become worse
4.	to experience wear and tear	D	to suffer damage resulting from ordinary use
5.	to become obsolete	E	to become outmoded
6.	to deplete	F	to reduce the amount of something, especially natural supply
7.	to accelerate	G	to increase the speed of
8.	recoverable amount	H	the highest value that can be obtained from an asset
9.	to spread out	I	to distribute evenly
10.	to impair	J	to perform impairment

UNIT 14

UNIT MAP

Reading 1	Classification of Intangible Assets
Reading 2	Valuation of Intangible Assets
Focus on Vocabulary	Intangible Assets Key Terms
Language Task	Intangible Assets and Company Performance
Focus on Grammar	Modals of Probability
Writing Task	Reporting on Company's Intangible Assets
Extra Activity 1	Answer the Questions *(see page 120)*

1. INTRODUCTION TO THE UNIT:

> Unit 14 examines intangible assets, which are the assets that lack physical substance (computer software, trademarks, patents, copyrights, etc.). Their importance in present days is far greater than it used to be in the past, since there are companies that own more in intangible assets than in property, plant and equipment.
>
> The first part of the Unit focuses on classification of intangible assets and accounting treatment of goodwill, a specific category of intangible assets. The second part of the Unit examines initial recognition of intangible assets and their subsequent measurement.

2. READING 1: Introduction

1. Apart from physical assets, what other types of assets do companies own?
   Assets that do not exist physically, i.e. intangible assets.

2. How can intangible assets be defined?
   Possible answer: *An asset that lacks physical substance.*

3. Why are in present days intangible assets far more important for companies and accountants than they were in the past?
   Possible answer: *In the past, large companies reported significant amounts of property and equipment on their balance sheets, but considerably smaller figures for intangible assets. Today, for many companies the situation is reverse.*

4. What are the examples of intangible assets?
   Patents; trademarks; computer software; databases; trade secrets; video and audio visual material; customer lists; licensing; royalty agreements; franchise agreements; copyrights; etc.

5. How can intangible assets be acquired?
   By separate purchase; as a part of business combination (i.e. through mergers and acquisitions); by self-creation (internal generation); by exchange of assets;

6. What are the examples of self-generated intangible assets?
   Possible answers: *Goodwill, brand name.*

7. How can intangible assets be classified?
   They are divided into two groups: legal intangibles and competitive intangibles.

8. What is the difference between the legal and competitive intangibles?
   Legal intangible assets can be legally owned, whereas competitive intangible assets cannot.

9. What are the examples of legal intangible assets?
   Patents, trademarks, internet domain names, trade secrets, customer lists purchased from other company.

10. What term denotes the violation of use of legal intangible assets?
    Infringement.

11. What are the examples of competitive intangible assets?
    Goodwill, brand recognition, know-how, business methodologies, human capital.

12. How do competitive intangible assets contribute to a company?
    They generate competitive advantage over the competitors.

13. What is goodwill in general terms?
    A company's good reputation or its customers' loyalty.

14. What is goodwill from the accounting point of view?
    In accounting, goodwill is an intangible asset that arises when one company acquires another, but pays more than the fair market value of the net assets.

3. READING COMPREHENSION 1: Answers

1. **How can an intangible asset be acquired?**
   Through a separate purchase, business combination, exchange or self-creation.

2. **What is the difference between legal and competitive intangibles?**
   Legal intangibles are considered property and their infringement can be defended in court, whereas competitive intangibles cannot be legally owned.

3. **How do competitive intangibles contribute to a company?**
   By providing an advantage over competitors, reducing costs and increasing effectiveness and revenues.

4. **What is goodwill in accounting terms?**
   An intangible asset that arises when one company acquires another, but pays more than the fair market value of the net assets.

Unit 14

READING 1 KEY VOCABULARY

intangible assets	patent	trademark
customer list	copyright	business combination
self-creation	internally generated	legal intangibles
competitive intangibles	intellectual property	infringement
trade secrets	franchise agreement	competitive advantage
goodwill	human capital	customers' loyalty

4. SPEAKING 1

Possible answers: Goodwill increases the equity value, creates the greater acquisition price in a takeover, increases the number of return clients based on their good experiences, creates opportunities for expansion, etc. Valuation of goodwill is difficult because of its vague nature and is often highly dependent on the judgment of the valuer. The true value of a company's goodwill becomes known only after the company is sold.

5. FOCUS ON VOCABULARY: Intangible Assets Key Terms

1. **intangible asset:** a non-physical asset having a useful life greater than one year.
2. **patent:** legal protection of an idea or invention.
3. **trademark:** a word, name, symbol, logo or other device identifying a product, officially registered and legally restricted to the use of the owner or manufacturer.
4. **copyright:** the legal right to control the production and selling of a book, play, film, photograph, or piece of music.
5. **infringement:** a breach of legal rights.
6. **legal intangible assets:** intellectual property such as trademarks, copyrights, patents, trade secrets, domain names, and goodwill.
7. **competitive intangible assets:** the source from which a company derives a competitive advantage, such as brand recognition, goodwill, know-how, business methodologies.
8. **royalty:** a share in the proceeds paid to an inventor or a proprietor for the right to use his or her invention or services.
9. **amortisation:** a gradual reduction of the value of an intangible asset
10. **goodwill:** the established reputation of a business regarded as a quantifiable asset.

Intangible Assets

6. LANGUAGE TASK

Students provide answers based on their company's resources. Alternatively, they may report on companies they have audited or whose accounts they have examined.

7. FOCUS ON GRAMMAR: Modals of Probability

Part 1: Possible answers:

1. The Company must (might, could) be undergoing restructuring.
2. The CEO must (might, could) have been involved in secret trading.
3. The due diligence must (might, could) have revealed some new facts.
4. The CAO must (might, could) have been implicated in fraudulent activities.

Additional Idea: You may vary the answers by stressing the fact that the CEO is a person of an undisputed integrity: *CEO can't have been implicated in fraudulent activities.*

8. READING 2: Introduction

1. When is an intangible asset recognised in a company's books?
   When it meets two criteria: when it is possible that a company will receive future economic benefits from the asset and when the asset can be measured reliably.

2. Why is it difficult to ascertain the market value of intangible property?
   Because it does not have a physical presence or easily determined value.

3. How are intangible assets initially recognised?
   They are initially measured at cost.

4. How are intangible assets measured after initial recognition?
   Usually under the cost model (at cost, minus accumulated amortisation), or alternatively under the revaluation model (at fair value, minus accumulated amortisation).

5. What is the fair value?
   The price that two parties are willing to pay in an active market in an arm's length transaction.

6. Why is the revaluation model rarely applied?
   Because there is no active market on which intangible assets trade (i.e. there is no possibility for comparison).

7. How do accountant acknowledge that the value of some intangible assets decreases over time?
   Intangible assets are subject to amortisation.

8. What is amortisation?
   The same process as depreciation, only applied to intangible assets.

9. What method is used to amortise intangible assets?
   Only the straight-line method.

10. How do accountants check whether the intangible asset is worth the amount stated on the balance sheet?
    By performing impairment testing.

11. Which financial statement reports gain or loss on disposal of an intangible asset?
    The profit and loss account.

9. READING COMPREHENSION 2: Answers

1. **Why is it difficult to estimate the market value of intangible assets?**
   Because they do not have a physical presence or an easily determined value.

2. **What are the recognition criteria for intangible assets?**
   An intangible asset is recognised when it is probable that the entity will receive future economic benefit from that asset and when the cost of the asset can be measured reliably.

3. **Why is it often difficult to apply the revaluation model?**
   Because there is no active market on which intangible assets trade.

4. **What is the aim of impairment testing?**
   To determine whether a balance sheet item is worth the amount stated on the balance sheet.

READING 2 KEY VOCABULARY

valuation	identifiable	cost model
revaluation model	amortisation	fair value
arm's length transaction	useful life	straight-line method
impairment	finite	to dispose of

10. SPEAKING 2

Students provide answers based on their company's practices.

11. WRITING TASK

Assign the writing task for homework.

12. BUILDING UP A NEW VOCABULARY

1. business combination	A. mergers and acquisitions
2. accumulated amortisation	B. the total sum of amortisation expense recorded for an intangible asset
3. to generate	C. to produce or create
4. to infringe	D. to violate
5. human capital	E. the skills, knowledge and experience that employees own, viewed in terms of their value to an organisation
6. brand recognition	F. the extent to which a consumer can correctly identify a particular product or service
7. to ascertain	G. to determine or discover definitely
8. revaluation model	H. an approach under which an intangible asset is measured at its fair value less accumulated amortisation
9. impairment	I. a permanent decline in the value of an asset
10. arm's length transaction	J. a transaction that takes place between two completely unrelated parties

UNIT 15

UNIT MAP

Reading 1	Audit Procedures
Reading 2	Audit Report
Focus on Vocabulary	Auditor's Terminology
Language Task	Audit Interview
Focus on Grammar	Reported Speech
Writing Task	Describing Audit Procedures
Extra Activity 1	Internal or External Auditor *(see page 121)*
Extra Activity 2	Audit Interview: Accounting Staff *(see Student's Book, page 137)*

1. INTRODUCTION TO THE UNIT

> Unit 15 focuses on audit, an official inspection of a company's records. The first part of the Unit examines audit objectives and procedures performed by an auditor. The second part of the Unit examines the content of an audit report and types of opinions issued by an auditor.

2. READING 1: Introduction

1. What is audit?
   An accounting procedure under which the financial records of a company are closely inspected to make sure that they are accurate.

2. Explain the difference between an internal and external auditor.
   An internal auditor works within an organisation and is responsible for evaluating accounting processes, risk management and internal controls. An external auditor conducts an independent examination of the accounts of an entity.

3. What qualifications and special training does an auditor need?
   The answers vary depending on the national requirements.

4. What business organisations are subject to mandatory audit?
   In most countries auditing is mandatory for large and medium-sized companies.

5. What is the objective of audit?
   To determine whether an organisation is providing a fair and accurate representation of its financial position.

6. What is the purpose of audit?
   To enforce accountability and enhance the degree of confidence of intended users of audit findings.

7. Who are the users of audit findings?
   Shareholders, regulatory and supervisory bodies, management, etc.

8. What does the audit procedure involve?
   The audit procedure involves an in-depth examination of physical and electronic records of an organisation by the auditor, including financial statements, receipts and invoices.

9. How does an auditor perform an audit in smaller organisations?
   The auditor examines the complete documentation.

10. How does an auditor select documents to be inspected in large companies?
    The auditor chooses documents through random sampling.

11. What does an auditor look for in financial statements?
    The auditor tries to determine if there are any discrepancies in financial reports, if any fraud occurred or if financial reports contain any anomalous entries, improprieties or clerical errors.

12. What does an auditor do during a financial audit?
    The auditor asks a range of questions, examines financial and accounting records, makes judgements on significant estimates or assumptions that management made, obtains written confirmation of certain matters, tests some of the organisation's internal control procedures, observes certain procedures being performed, etc.

13. How does the management respond to irregularities detected during an audit?
    In response, the management makes material adjustments (i.e. corrections) and records them as requested by the auditor.

14. What attitude should auditors assume when performing an audit?
    An audit should be performed with an attitude of professional scepticism.

3. READING COMPREHENSION 1: Answers

1. **What is audit?**
   An accounting procedure under which the financial records of a company are closely inspected to make sure that they are accurate.

2. **What is the objective of audit?**
   To determine whether an organisation provides a fair and accurate representation of its financial position.

3. **What is the purpose of audit?**
   To enforce accountability and enhance the degree of confidence of intended users in financial statements.

4. **What third parties are interested in audit findings?**
   Shareholders, management, regulatory bodies, lenders and other people with an interest in the health of the company.

Unit 15

READING 1 KEY VOCABULARY

statutory	mandatory	threshold
accountability	regulatory body	in-depth examination
random sampling	discrepancy	impropriety
anomalous entry	clerical error	material adjustment
disclosure	estimate	assumption
approximation	misstatement	scepticism

4. SPEAKING 1

Students provide answers based on their audit experiences.

5. FOCUS ON VOCABULARY: Auditor's Terminology

1. When an auditor issues this opinion, you needn't worry. Everything is fine with your company's financial records: **Unqualified Opinion**

2. When an auditor issues this opinion, you should be slightly worried. However, except for certain issues, your company's financial records are fine: **Qualified Opinion**

3. When an auditor issues this opinion, the situation is not good. Your company's financial records contain major flows or the auditor thinks your company might not remain in business for long: **Adverse Opinion**

4. This means that an auditor cannot express an opinion because of lack of relevant facts: **Disclaimer of Opinion**

5. This is a paragraph in auditor's opinion in which users' attention is drawn to an issue of particular importance: **Emphasis of Matter**

6. A type of attitude where nothing is taken for granted: **Professional Scepticism**

7. Inaccuracy in financial statements that may affect the economic decisions of the users of financial statements: **Material Misstatement**

8. Correction of a fundamental error: **Material Adjustment**

9. An item that deviates from normal or standard: **Anomalous Entry**

10. Inconsistency or difference between things that should be the same: **Discrepancy**

6. LANGUAGE TASK

Before doing the exercise, ask students what are the typical questions that an auditor might ask. Give time to prepare questions and answers.

7. FOCUS ON GRAMMAR

Students use the answers from the previous exercise to relate the content of an audit interview.

8. READING 2: Introduction

1. What is an audit report?
   A written opinion of an auditor regarding an entity's financial statements.

2. How many paragraphs does an audit report usually have?
   Three: the introductory, the scope and the opinion paragraph.

3. What information does the each paragraph contain?
   The introductory paragraph: *the responsibility of the auditor and the company's management.*
   The scope paragraph: *the description of work the auditor performed.*
   The opinion paragraph: *the reference to the financial reporting framework used for preparing financial statements and the auditor's opinion.*

4. Why might an auditor include the 'emphasis of matter' paragraph?
   Because the auditor considers it necessary to draw the users' attention to a matter disclosed in the financial statements that is of fundamental importance for their understanding.

5. What type of opinions can an auditor issue?
   An unqualified, qualified and adverse opinion.
   Note: In the auditing context, the word 'qualified' means limited or restricted.

6. When does an auditor issue an unqualified opinion?
   When financial statements present a fair and accurate picture of the company and comply with the relevant accounting principles.

7. When does an auditor issue a qualified opinion?
   When the auditor concludes that misstatements are material, but not pervasive to the financial statements.

8. When does an auditor issue an adverse opinion?
   It is issued when the auditor concludes that misstatements are both material and pervasive to the financial statements.

9. What happens if an auditor is unable to obtain relevant facts necessary for issuing an opinion?
   An auditor issues a disclaimer of opinion, which is an auditor's statement disclaiming any opinion regarding the company's financial condition.

Unit 15

10. What expression do auditors use to say that financial statements present an objective picture of a company's financial condition?
    *They say that financial statements present a **true and fair view** of a company's financial condition.*

11. What rules and professional principles must auditors adhere to in their work?
    Ethical principles, adherence to standards of auditing and professional scepticism.

12. What ethical principles should auditors be governed by?
    Independence, integrity, objectivity and confidentiality.

9. READING COMPREHENSION 2: Answers

1. **What elements make up an audit report?**
   An audit report usually consists of three paragraphs: the opening, the scope and the opinion paragraph.

2. **What are the reasons for including the emphasis of matter paragraph?**
   The reason is that the auditor considers it necessary to draw the users' attention to a matter disclosed in the financial statements that is of fundamental importance for their understanding.

3. **What type of opinions does an auditor issue?**
   An auditor may issue an unqualified, qualified or adverse opinion.

4. **What is a disclaimer of opinion?**
   An auditor's statement disclaiming any opinion regarding the company's financial condition.

   Note: to 'disclaim' means to decline to accept the responsibility for something

READING 2 KEY VOCABULARY

reporting framework	emphasis of matter	unqualified opinion
qualified opinion	material	pervasive
adverse opinion	misstatement	going-concern
disclaimer of opinion	true and fair view	fair presentation

10. SPEAKING 2

Encourage students to relate the answers to their own experiences, either as accountants or auditors. Let them speak freely and do not overcorrect.

11. WRITING TASK

Assign the writing task for homework.

12. BUILDING UP A NEW VOCABULARY

1. statutory	A required by the government
2. random sampling	B a method in which all members of a group have an equal chance of being selected
3. impropriety	C something that is wrong or unacceptable according to moral, social, or professional standards
4. clerical error	D an unintentional mistake
5. assumption	E a statement that is presumed to be true without concrete evidence to support it
6. approximation	F an estimate of the value of something
7. pervasive	G in auditing, something that is material to more than one of the primary financial statements
8. true and fair view	H words used by auditors to show that they think the accounts give correct and complete information about a company's financial situation
9. bias	I preference or prejudice for or against one person
10. integrity	J the quality of being honest and having strong moral principles

Extra Activities

UNIT 1 Extra Activity 1:
Gap Filling

1. Fill in the gaps with words from the box below.

specialising	for inspecting its accounts
giving administrative support	studying
processing the records	to inspect its accounts

Trainee Accountants
   Accountants who are _____ for professional examinations.

Bookkeepers
   Administrative staff responsible for _____ of a company's financial activities.

Tax Accountant
   An accountant _____ in a company's tax affairs.

Back-Office Manager
   Person in charge of the staff responsible for _____ to the Finance Department.

Internal Auditors
   Employees of a company who are responsible for _____.

External Auditors
   People employed by an outside firm of accountants and hired by a company _____.

UNIT 1 Extra Activity 2:
Rank the Skills and Qualities

Rank the skills and qualities according to their importance and add three you find particularly important.

1. numerical and analytical skills	
2. the ability to communicate well	
3. the ability to interpret and clearly explain complex issues	
4. the ability to conduct and accurately interpret research	
5. integrity	
6. problem solving skills	
7. self-confidence	
8. diplomacy	
9. excellent written, verbal and presentation skills	
10. the ability to work in a team	
11. responsibility	
12. adaptability	
13.	
14.	
15.	

UNIT 1 Extra Activity 3:
English Analysis

Discuss the questions:

1. In your opinion, what is the most difficult part of English?
   - grammar
   - vocabulary
   - pronunciation
   - understanding authentic texts
   - communication with native speakers
   - other

2. How often do you use English in your job?

3. How do you meet English regularly?
   - read professional literature
   - through contact with native speakers
   - private reading
   - other

4. What do you need English for?
   - talk about figures
   - make small talks
   - make presentations
   - read business correspondence
   - write reports
   - discuss proposals
   - talk on the phone
   - communicate with native speakers
   - read professional literature

UNIT 2 Extra Activity 1:
What functions do you perform?

Pair work: Students interview each other and present their findings.

FUNCTION	YOU	YOUR COLLEAGUE
post journal entries		
fill in tax returns		
produce invoices		
interpret financial data to the company management		
prepare financial statements		
monitor tax legislation		
maintain the general ledger		
count inventory		
review and inspect financial records		
review compliance with tax regulations		
analyse the company's financial position		
produce estimates of the company's annual budget		

UNIT 2 Extra Activity 2:
Analysing Different Forms of Business Organisations

Discuss positive and negative aspects of different business organisations.

	Sole Proprietorship	Partnership	Private Limited Company	Public Limited Company
formation expense				
operating expense				
tax aspect				
control over organisation				
liability for debts				
ability to raise capital				
management simplicity				

UNIT 2 Extra Activity 3:
Setting Up a Business

You are about to set up your own business. Consider the possible revenues and expenses, as well as all other aspects of your business operations. Think of the following:

1. Legal Form
    - sole proprietorship
    - partnership (general or limited)
    - private limited company
    - public limited company

2. Type of Services / Products Provided

3. Business Premises

4. Equipment

5. Budget
    - identify the source of start-up and operating capital
    - estimate monthly operating costs
    - estimate the projected revenue
    - estimate the break-even point

6. Potential Market
    - identify your market and client potential
    - identify your competitive advantages
    - target group
    - niche market

7. Marketing
    - how to reach prospective clients
    - means of advertising

8. Work Experience

9. Family Back-Up

10. Any other aspect of your business

UNIT 3 Extra Activity 1:
Verb-Noun Stress Patterns

Complete the sentence pairs with the appropriate form of the words in the box.

| discount | upgrade | export | record | subject |
| decrease | conduct | refund | research | permit |

1. She had to check the company _____.
   Her job is to _____ transactions.

2. We have seen a _____ in sales this year.
   Sales are _____ every year.

3. Oil is our major _____.
   They _____ oil to the UK.

4. The company offers a _____ if you buy more than a certain amount.
   They are _____ all merchandise.

5. I'd like a _____ please. This sweater doesn't fit me.
   They _____ her 50% of the price.

6. Do you need a _____ to import these goods?
   They don't _____ to import more than one bottle of alcoholic drinks.

7. The air company offered them a flight _____.
   The company _____ its software.

8. His _____ was unacceptable.
   They _____ a survey on financial accounting practices.

9. He published his new _____ in the academic journal.
   He _____ the effects of new economic measures.

10. What _____ do you study?
    She was _____ to harsh criticism.

UNIT 4 Extra Activity 1: Identify the Cost

STUDENT A

Identify the cost your partner describes. Add two examples of your own.

STUDENT A	STUDENT B
1. accounting fees	1.
2. legal fees	2.
3. safety costs	3.
4. office supplies	4.
5. insurance	5.
6. depreciation	6.
7. travel expense	7.
8. lease	8.
9. packaging	9.
10. sales commissions	10.
11. sick leave pay	11.
12. research and development costs	12.
13. interests	13.
14.	14.
15.	15.

UNIT 4 Extra Activity 1: Identify the Cost

STUDENT B

Identify the cost your partner describes. Add two examples of your own.

STUDENT A	STUDENT B
1.	1. bank charges
2.	2. utilities
3.	3. maintenance costs
4.	4. advertising costs
5.	5. maternity allowance
6.	6. fringe benefits
7.	7. corporate entertainment
8.	8. property tax
9.	9. shipping costs
10.	10. warehousing
11.	11. severance pay
12.	12. warranties
13.	13. income tax payable
14.	14.
15.	15.

UNIT 4 Extra Activity 2: Check Your Figures

STUDENT A

Read out the numbers in your column. Check if they match with your partner's numbers.

	STUDENT A	STUDENT B
1.	7,563,987	
2.	231, 689,409	
3.	14.07.1998 (date)	
4.	$ 376,546	
5.	0.112 cm	
6.	Tel: 00 381 11 21 34 44	
7.	7/10 mile	
8.	97.5%	
9.	3,645,845,879	
10.	11.3.1900 (date)	
11.	£ 34.75	
12.	124/200	
13.	3/4 hour	
14.	27.11.2001 (date)	
15.	€ 72,562	

UNIT 4 Extra Activity 2: Check Your Figures

STUDENT B

Read out the numbers in your column. Check if they match with your partner's numbers.

STUDENT A	STUDENT B
	1. 7,563,887
	2. 231,789,409
	3. 14.06.1998 (date)
	4. $ 376,546
	5. 0.113 cm
	6. Tel: 00 381 11 21 34 44
	7. 7/9 mile
	8. 87.5 %
	9. 3,645,845,879
	10. 11.4.1900
	11. £ 54.75
	12. 224/200
	13. 3/6 hour
	14. 27.11.2001 (date)
	15. € 82,562

UNIT 5 Extra Activity 1:
Income Statement Entries

STUDENT A

Ask questions to complete the income statement entries.

Account Number	ITEM	2010	2011	THIS YEAR
1	**SALES REVENUE**	€ 700,000		€ 900,000
2	COSTS OF MATERIAL	€ 300,000	€ 250,000	
3	LABOUR COST	€ 200,000		€ 250,000
4	**TOTAL COST OF GOODS SOLD**	€ 500,000	€ 450,000	
5	**GROSS MARGIN**	€ 200,000		€ 300,000
6	TRAVEL EXPENSES	€ 20,000	€ 15,000	
7	LEGAL COSTS	€ 10,000		€ 10,000
8	UTILITIES	€ 60,000	€ 60,000	
9	**TOTAL GENERAL AND ADMINISTRATIVE EXPENSES**	€ 90,000		€ 100,000
10	**OPERATING MARGIN**	€ 110,000	€ 65,000	
11	TAXES	€ 15,000		€ 30,000
12	**NET INCOME**	€ 95,000	€ 50,000	

UNIT 5 Extra Activity 1:
Income Statement Entries

STUDENT B

Ask questions to complete the income statement entries.

Account Number	ITEM	2010	2011	THIS YEAR
1	**SALES REVENUE**	€ 700,000	€ 600,000	
2	COSTS OF MATERIAL	€ 300,000		€ 350,000
3	LABOUR COST	€ 200,000	€ 200,000	
4	**TOTAL COST OF GOODS SOLD**	€ 500,000		€ 600,000
5	**GROSS MARGIN**	€ 200,000	€ 150,000	
6	TRAVEL EXPENSES	€ 20,000		€ 30,000
7	LEGAL COSTS	€ 10,000	€ 10,000	
8	UTILITIES	€ 60,000		€ 60,000
9	**TOTAL GENERAL AND ADMINISTRATIVE EXPENSES**	€ 90,000	€ 85,000	
10	**OPERATING MARGIN**	€ 110,000		€ 200,000
11	TAXES	€ 15,000	€ 15,000	
12	**NET INCOME**	€ 95,000		€ 170,000

UNIT 5 Extra Activity 2:
Preparing an Income Statement

List all your company's revenues and expenses and prepare a brief income statement. Present it to your partner and compare the business results. Suggest how the business performance of your partner's company can be improved.

UNIT 5 Extra Activity 3:
Various Expenses

Discuss how much your company spends on the following expenses:

- sales commissions:
- bonuses:
- client entertainment:
- advertising expense:
- lease of premises:
- shipping and handling fees:
- warehousing:
- packaging:
- licences and permits:
- legal fees:
- utilities expense:
- depreciation of equipment:
- warranty expenses:
- office supplies:
- sundry (miscellaneous) expenses:

UNIT 6 Extra Activity 1:
Determining a Company's Assets and Liabilities

STUDENT 1: You are a company accountant. Your CAO asked you to list the company's assets and liabilities. Consider the items in the box or any other that you find relevant.

STUDENT 2: You are a Chief Accounting Officer. A potential investor wants information on your company's financial position. Interview your accountant to determine the company's net worth.

cash and cash equivalents	short-term borrowings	government securities
property plant and equipment	accounts payable	insurance liability
goodwill	trademarks	accounts receivable
dividends payable	inventories	long-term borrowings
prepaid expenses	marketable securities	accrued expenses

ASSETS	LIABILITIES
Current Assets	**Current Liabilities**
Non-Current Assets	**Non-Current Liabilities**
Intangible Assets	
Total Assets:	**Total Liabilities:**
Shareholders' Equity:	

UNIT 6 Extra Activity 2: Interviewing a Candidate

Your company is hiring a new junior corporate accountant. You are in charge of interviewing applicants. Find out about their previous experience by asking questions as presented in the example below. Add some questions of your own.

Example: *Have you ever worked as a corporate accountant?*

	Activity	Yes/No
1.	outline policies, procedures and internal regulations	
2.	carry out internal audit engagements	
3.	manage accounting for inventory, accounts receivable and payable	
4.	prepare financial statements and supporting financial information	
5.	respond to queries from external auditors	
6.	conduct training and development programmes for employees	
7.	examine legal loopholes	
8.	monitor legislation and regulations	
9.	prepare a tax balance	
10.	prepare budget to allocate funds for spending in each department	
11.		
12.		
13.		
14.		
15.		

UNIT 7 Extra Activity 1:
Why Small Companies Fail

Discuss in pairs reasons why small companies often fail. Consider the items below and other possible causes. Think of specific examples you are familiar with. Suggest solutions to the problems listed.

- lack of capital (cash flow problems)
- inability to get sufficient capital to expand
- intense competition
- unsound business plan
- inability to do market research
- poor managerial skills
- other

UNIT 7 Extra Activity 2:
Cash Flow Problems

STUDENT A

You run a small business and seemingly doing fine. However, you are experiencing cash flow problems. Ask your accountant to help you.

1. **Consider the following aspects of your business:**

   - type of products / services you provide
   - how much you charge for your product/service
   - how long it takes you to make the product / provide the services
   - terms of payment you offer to customers
   - how much you pay for supplies
   - terms of payment your suppliers offer you
   - number of employees you have
   - how much you pay for salaries and wages
   - any other aspect of your business you find relevant to your problem

2. **Discuss the suggestions your accountant has made. Decide which are applicable and which are not.**

UNIT 7 Extra Activity 2: Cash Flow Problem

STUDENT B

You are a CPA. Your client needs help with a cash-flow problem.

1. **Ask your client about the following aspects of his/her business:**

    - type of product or service he/she provides
    - how much he/she charges for the product/service
    - how long it takes him/her to make the product / provide the services
    - terms of payment he/she offers to customers
    - how much he/she pays for supplies
    - terms of payment the suppliers offer to your client
    - number of employees he/she has
    - how much he/she pays for salaries and wages
    - any other aspect of his/her business you find relevant to his/her problem

UNIT 7 Extra Activity 3: Shareholders' Equity

Complete the sentences with the words from the box

dividends	unrealised gain or loss	comprehensive income
opening balance	additional paid-in capital	par value (nominal value)
closing balance	treasury shares	retained earnings
share capital		

1. _____ is the amount at the beginning of accounting period.
2. _____ is the amount at the end of accounting period.
3. _____ is the amount of money that a company received in exchange for company shares.
4. _____ represent the amount of the net income retained by a company for reinvestment in its operations and not distributed in form of dividends.
5. _____ represent the amount of net earnings distributed to shareholders proportional to the number of shares owned.
6. _____ is the price of shares at which they were initially issued by a company, unrelated to its market price.
7. _____ is the value of a company's shares that is above the value at which they were initially issued.
8. _____ are shares bought back or held by a company.
9. _____ is a gain (or loss) that exists on paper and is not realised until the underlying asset is sold.
10. _____ is the sum of net income and other items that are not recognised in income statement because they have not been realised.

UNIT 8 Extra Activity 1:
Creating a More Effective Tax Strategy

STUDENT A

You are a tax consultant engaged by a large company to create a more effective tax strategy. You will be interviewing a company's CAO. Ask questions to find out how you might help. Consider the following:

- tax incentives
- tax deductions
- transfer pricing
- outsourcing
- legal loopholes
- offshore tax havens
- any other issue relevant to the tax strategy

Present some preliminary ideas.

UNIT 8 Extra Activity 1:
Creating a More Effective Tax Strategy

STUDENT B

You are a Chief Accounting Officer of a large company. Your company has engaged a tax consultant to create a more effective tax strategy. He/she will be interviewing you. Consider the following:

- tax incentives
- tax deductions
- transfer pricing
- outsourcing
- legal loopholes
- off shore tax havens
- any other issue relevant to tax strategy

Discuss the proposals the tax consultant has made.

UNIT 8 Extra Activity 2:
Describing a Taxable Event

Work in pairs:

STUDENT 1: Describe a situation causing a taxable event.
STUDENT 2: Say what tax is imposed.

Example:
   Student 1: A person bought a painting for $ 5,000 and sold it later for $ 20,000.
   Student 2: Capital gains tax

1	
2	
3	
4	
5	

UNIT 8 Extra Activity 3:
Doing Business in Your Country

STUDENT A

As a potential investor, you are interested in various aspects of your partner's country taxation system and general conditions for doing business. Find out about the issues presented below:

- main forms of business organisations
- business regulations
- sources of business finance
- investment incentives
- government grants
- tax system
- principal taxes
- current corporate income tax rate
- local taxes
- social security contributions
- tax allowances
- tax exemptions
- tax credits
- tax incentives
- transfer pricing
- double taxation treaties

UNIT 8 Extra Activity 3:
Doing Business in Your Country

STUDENT B

You are a tax consultant. A foreign investor needs information on various aspects of your country's taxation system and general conditions for doing business. Prepare answers to the issues presented below:

- main forms of business organisations
- business regulations
- sources of business finance
- investment incentives
- government grants
- tax system
- principal taxes
- current corporate income tax rate
- local taxes
- social security contributions
- tax allowances
- tax exemptions
- tax credits
- tax incentives
- transfer pricing
- double taxation treaties

UNIT 9 Extra Activity 1: Completing an Invoice

Company Name: _____
Street: _____
Postcode / Place / Country: _____
Tax Identification Number: _____
Company Registration Number: _____
Bank Account / Bank Name: _____
Telephone / Fax: _____
Email: _____

INVOICE No: _____ INVOICE TO: _____
Invoice date: _____ COMPANY NAME: _____
Invoice place: _____ Address, Postcode: _____
Delivery date: _____ Tax ID: _____
Payment terms: _____

SHIP TO: _____

COMPANY NAME: _____

Address, Postcode: _____

No	Description	Quantity	Unit of Measurement	Unit Price	Amount without VAT	VAT %	VAT Amount	Amount with VAT
1.								
2.								
3.								
4.								
5.								

TOTAL AMOUNT: _____

UNIT 9 Extra Activity 2:
Dealing with Overdue Accounts

STUDENT A: Cash Collection Officer

You are a cash collection officer. Your company has issued several invoices, (now long overdue), to a client and you try to recover the cash. Although the amount of debt is quite high, you would like to avoid taking legal action and prefer to have it settled without direct confrontation with the client. Call the client.

STUDENT B: Client

You have received several invoices from your supplier, which you have not paid yet. You are experiencing cash flow problems and would like to avoid payment as long as possible. However, you don't want to be sued and prefer to maintain good relationship with the supplier. You are expecting a call from the supplier.

UNIT 10 Extra Activity 1:
Name the Accounting Principle

Explain how the business event is reflected in the company business records or financial statements. Name the relevant accounting principle where applicable.

1. The owner of a company personally acquires an office building and rents the space in it to his company at $ 5,000 per month.
2. An item in inventory has a cost of $ 20, but it can be replaced for $ 15.
3. A company is involved in a lawsuit, which it is likely to lose.
4. A company is involved in a lawsuit, which it is likely to win.
5. You are an accountant. Your client claims he has a receipt for a purchase he made, but he is unable to find it.
6. A company has net assets worth $ 10 million. Customer A, who owes $ 1,000 to the Company, defaults.
7. Under a bonus plan, an employee earns a $10,000 bonus based on measurable aspects of his performance within the current year. The bonus is paid in the following year.
8. A company is exhibiting indicators such as defaulting on its loans, incurring significant trading losses, has a rising level of short-term overdrafts not supported by operational growth. In addition, it faces a number of legal proceedings.
9. The tax rate is expected to change in near future.

UNIT 11 Extra Activity 1:
Real Life Crimes

Identify the crime committed:

1. Contracting officers were accused of accepting money in return for steering multi-million dollar contracts to certain companies.
2. A financial institution employee diverted funds from legitimate accounts into "dummy" accounts.
3. An accounts payable clerk used his computer to access the company's accounting software without authorisation and issued various cheques payable to himself.
4. A company's false financial reporting caused a subsequent loss to investors amounting to US$11 billion.
5. A town mayor used public funds to build his private house.
6. A customer was invoiced for 100 boxes, but only 98 actually arrived.
7. A film star has been caught 'borrowing' items from a shop.
8. An employee has been caught taking stamps and paper from work.
9. A company published a book without paying for the copyrights.
10. A corporate manager sold an overseas corporate real estate asset at a fraction of its market value to a front company that he owned.

UNIT 11 Extra Activity 2:
Accounting Frauds

Match the accounting fraud to the area it is related to:

| accounts receivable | inventory | liability and expense | assets |

1. not recording customer warranty claims _____
2. recording fictitious revenues (related parties, consignment or sham sales) _____
3. not writing off uncollectable debts _____
4. manipulating cash received from related parties as cash received from customers _____
5. overvaluation of finished goods _____
6. not recording contingent liabilities _____
7. not writing off obsolete stock items _____
8. overstating assets through mergers and acquisitions _____
9. recording fictitious inventory _____
10. not recording accounts payable _____
11. understating provision for doubtful debts _____
12. overstating marketable securities _____
13. failing to record depreciation / amortisation expense _____
14. under-recording purchases _____
15. over-counting physical inventory _____
16. not recording accrued expense _____

UNIT 11 Extra Activity 3:
Internal Control Measures

Explain how the internal control measure listed below can minimise error, deter fraud, theft and dishonest behaviour against the organisation.

- control over information processing
- segregation of duties
- access restriction to resources and records
- physical control over vulnerable assets
- reconciliation
- inspection of incoming shipment before making payment to suppliers
- appropriate documentation of transactions

UNIT 12 Extra Activity 1:
Identify the Timing Difference

1. A company pays $ 30,000 rent payment in December for the period from January to June of the following year.
2. A restaurant paid an annual franchise fee in October 2017 for the following year.
3. An IT maintenance company repaired a customer's computer two months ago. The customer paid the invoice by the end of the next month.
4. Financial News Magazine sells subscription to their magazine, which is published 12 times a year. The annual subscription costs $ 250.
5. In 2017, a company bought a truck for $ 12,000. They expect it to last 5 years. The company records an annual depreciation expense at $ 2,000.
6. A company received a rent payment for the next six months' occupancy.
7. A company paid advertising costs for the campaign that will last 6 months.
8. In October, a company received cash in advance of rendering services. A half of the services will be provided by 31 December.
9. In May 2017, a company sold goods worth $ 5,000 on credit. It should receive the payment in the following year.
10. A company paid $ 12,000 insurance premium in December. The insurance protection covers the period from January to June of the following year.

UNIT 12 Extra Activity 2:
Ethical Dilemmas

Work with a partner. Think of ethical dilemmas that accountants face in course of their work. Describe a possible scenario and ask your partner how he or she would react in a given situation.

Consider the following issues:

- conflict of interests
- clients who request manipulation of financial statements
- pressure from the management to inflate earnings
- confidentiality of information
- tax evasion
- transfer pricing
- creative accounting
- money laundering
- fraudulent activities

UNIT 13 Extra Activity 1: Calculating Depreciation

1. **Case Study 1:**

   A company has bought a machine worth $ 100,000 for its new plant. The estimated useful life of the machine is 10 years. Use the terms below to explain how depreciation expense is calculated:

useful life	historical cost	depreciable amount
estimated residual value	depreciation rate	recovery period

   Calculate the book value of the equipment after three years of use.

2. **Case Study 2: Straight Line Method**

   A fixed asset having a useful life of 3 years is purchased on 1 January 2016. The cost of the asset is $ 2,000, whereas its residual value is expected to be $ 500. Calculate the depreciation expense for the year ending on 30 June 2016.

3. **Case Study 3: Accelerated Method**

   A company purchased several new computers for their staff. The purchase value of the computers is $ 10,000. Computers do not have a long useful life; however, five years is a realistic and adequate period.
   Computers also deteriorate in value much quicker in the first year than in the later years so the accelerated depreciation method is more appropriate. At the end of five years, computers are generally worthless, so the salvage value will be $ 0. Depreciate the asset by using the accelerated method: 40% in the first year.

UNIT 13 Extra Activity 2:
Causes of Depreciation

Work with a partner. Describe a situation illustrating one of the causes of depreciation listed below. Your partner should guess what you are describing.

- wear and tear
- deterioration
- obsolescence
- inadequacy
- depletion of natural resource

UNIT 14 Extra Activity 1:
Answer the Questions

Answer the questions by using the phrases from the box:

trademark infringement	an application for a patent	goodwill
a design registration	an application for a trademark	customer list
royalty	an application for a copyright registration	

Question 1:

Your company has developed a unique new product (a device or machine), which is based on an entirely new concept. How do you protect your product from being copied by competition?

You file _____

Question 2:

You have invented a new form of product packaging and you want to protect it from being copied. How do you protect the external appearance of the product from being copied by competition?

You file _____

Question 3:

You sell a distinctive, quality product and want the customers to recognise your brand and do not confuse it with competitors' products. How do you ensure that?

You file _____

Question 4:

Your record label wants to protect its songs from being illegally downloaded or reproduced. What do you do?

You file _____

Question 5:

A competitor has been unlawfully using your trademark. You decide to take a legal action against what offence?

_____

Question 6

Being a trade company, this is your company's most valuable asset. Protecting this asset is possible under the trade secret law. What is the asset in question?

_____

Question 7

You have decided to sell your company. The fair market value of your company's net assets is estimated at $ 8 million. However, the acquirer had to pay $ 9 million. On account of what asset were you able to increase the price of your company?

_____

Question 8

What is the name of the payment made to an owner for the use of property, especially patents, copyrighted works, franchises or natural resources?

_____

UNIT 15 Extra Activity 1:
Internal Or External Auditor

Look at the following activities and decide which are normally done internally or externally.

1. spends time getting to know the business, as well as the environment and the industry in which it operates
2. analyses the internal business and financial systems used to make and record transactions
3. gathers evidence on the business methods and transactions of the company
4. gives advice on the business methods and transactions of the company
5. examines financial statements to determine whether they conform to relevant accounting principles
6. examines the management report and determines whether it conforms to the financial statements
7. guarantees the correctness of the figures presented in the accounts
8. provides consulting services
9. presents a written report to the management of the company, describing whether the accounting records, financial statements and management reports conform to legal requirements
10. maintains confidentiality and independence

UNIT 15 Extra Activity 2:
Audit Interview – Accounting Staff

Part 1

If you were an auditor, what questions would you ask an accounting staff person to detect possible fraud or any other illegal activity?

Part 2

Use your ideas and the prompts below to prepare questions for an audit interview. Interview your partner and present your opinion based on the obtained answers.

- time with the company
- accounting duties
- accounting department / sufficient staff
- existence of internal controls to prevent, deter and detect fraudulent recording of transactions
- supervisor communicating his views on ethical behaviour
- existence of procedure for informing superiors in case of suspicion of fraudulent activities
- any awareness of unauthorised persons gaining access to the accounting system
- transactions recorded after the close of business or during the weekend
- ever requested by superiors to record unusual, undocumented transaction
- ethical standards demonstrated by colleagues, supervisors, senior management
- most likely way to record fraudulent transactions
- most likely person to record fraudulent transactions
- aware of allegations that that fraudulent journal entries have been recorded
- aware of any allegations that fraud has been committed
- you perpetrated fraud against the company

Extra Activities: The Key

UNIT 1

EXTRA ACTIVITY 1: The Key

1. Fill in the gaps with words from the box below.

specialising	for inspecting its accounts	giving administrative support
studying	processing the records	to inspect its accounts

Trainee Accountants
Accountants who are **studying** for professional examinations.

Bookkeepers
Administrative staff responsible for **processing the records** of a company's financial activities.

Tax Accountant
An accountant **specialising** in a company's tax affairs.

Back-Office Manager
Person in charge of the staff responsible for **giving administrative support** to the Finance Department.

Internal Auditors
Employees of a company who are responsible for **inspecting its accounts**.

External Auditors
People employed by an outside firm of accountants and hired by a **company to inspect its accounts.**

EXTRA ACTIVITY 2

Students work in pairs and report on their partner. Ask students to provide arguments for their choices and the context. *Example: Why do you need to be diplomatic in your job?*

EXTRA ACTIVITY 3

Students work in pairs and report on their partner. Use this opportunity to learn about their language needs and ask them to provide the context for their answers.

UNIT 2

EXTRA ACTIVITY 1

Students work in pairs and report on their partner. The purpose of the exercise is to introduce the key accounting verbs and practise Present Simple Tense. When the pair work is completed, students report on their findings. *Example: Mark posts journal entries, but he doesn't monitor tax legislation.*

EXTRA ACTIVITY 2

Students discuss individual aspects of different business organisations. The purpose of the exercise to provide an opportunity for students to practise vocabulary related to business organisations and fully understand the differences between them.

EXTRA ACTIVITY 3

Divide students into groups. Leave students to decide on a type of business they want to set up and let them work on their own. When they finish, they present their project to the class. Students from other groups play a devil's advocate, i.e. ask questions in order to identify weak points in their plans.

UNIT 3

EXTRA ACTIVITY 1: The Key

1. She had to check the company records.
   Her job is to **record transactions**.

2. We have seen a decrease in sales this year.
   Sales are **decreasing** every year.

3. Oil is our major export.
   They **export** oil to the UK.

4. The company offers a discount if you buy more than a certain amount.
   They are **discounting** all merchandise.

5. I'd like a refund please. This sweater doesn't fit me.
   They **refunded** her 50% of the price.

6. Do you need a permit to import these goods?
   They don't **permit** to import more than one bottle of alcoholic drinks.

7. The air company offered them a flight upgrade.
   The company **upgraded** its software.

8. His conduct was unacceptable.
   They **conducted** a survey on financial accounting practices.

9. He published his new research in the academic journal.
   He **researched** the effects of new economic measures.

10. What subjects do you study?
    She was **subjected** to harsh criticism.

UNIT 4

EXTRA ACTIVITY 1: The Key

STUDENT A	STUDENT B
1. accounting fees	1. bank charges
2. legal fees	2. utilities
3. safety costs	3. maintenance costs
4. office supplies	4. advertising costs
5. insurance	5. maternity allowance
6. depreciation	6. fringe benefits
7. travel expense	7. corporate entertainment
8. lease	8. property tax
9. packaging	9. shipping costs
10. sales commissions	10. warehousing
11. sick leave pay	11. severance pay
12. research and development costs	12. warranties
13. interests	13. income tax payable
14.	14.
15.	15.

UNIT 4

EXTRA ACTIVITY 2: The Key

1. 7,563,987	1. 7,563,887
2. 231,689,409	2. 231,789,409
3. 14.07.1998 (date)	3. 14.06.1998 (date)
4. $ 376,546	4. $ 376,546
5. 0.112 cm	5. 0.113 cm
6. Tel: 00 381 11 21 34 44	6. Tel: 00 381 11 21 34 44
7. 7/10 mile	7. 7/9 mile
8. 97.5%	8. 87.5%
9. 3,645,845,879	9. 3,645,845,879
10. 11.3.1900 (date)	10. 11.4.1900 (date)
11. £ 34.75	11. £ 54.75
12. 124/200	12. 224/200
13. 3/4 hour	13. 3/6 hour
14. 27.11.2001 (date)	14. 27.11.2001 (date)
15. € 72,562	15. € 82,562

UNIT 5

EXTRA ACTIVITY 1: The Key

Students ask questions to complete the income statement entries.

Additional idea: After completing the missing information, this exercise can be used for a comparative practice of the Past Simple and the Present Perfect Tense.

Example: *How much did the sales revenue decrease in 2011 in comparison to 2010?*
It decreased by € 100,000.

How much has the sales revenue increased this year?
It has increased by € 300,000.

Account Number	ITEM	2010	2011	THIS YEAR
1	SALES REVENUE	€ 700,000	€ 600,000	€ 900,000
2	COSTS OF MATERIAL	€ 300,000	€ 250,000	€ 350,000
3	LABOUR COST	€ 200,000	€ 200,000	€ 250,000
4	TOTAL COST OF GOODS SOLD	€ 500,000	€ 450,000	€ 600,000
5	GROSS MARGIN	€ 200,000	€ 150,000	€ 300,000
6	TRAVEL EXPENSES	€ 20,000	€ 15,000	€ 30,000
7	LEGAL COSTS	€ 10,000	€ 10,000	€ 10,000
8	UTILITIES	€ 60,000	€ 60,000	€ 60,000
9	TOTAL GENERAL AND ADMINISTRATIVE EXPENSES	€ 90,000	€ 85,000	€ 100,000
10	OPERATING MARGIN	€ 110,000	€ 65,000	€ 200,000
11	TAXES	€ 15,000	€ 15,000	€ 30,000
12	NET INCOME	€ 95,000	€ 50,000	€ 170,000

UNIT 5

EXTRA ACTIVITIES 2 AND 3

Extra Activities 2 & 3 might be merged into one. Divide students into groups. Let them think of an imaginary company or the one they have audited or whose accounts they have examined. The group providing financial advice might use list of expenses in Extra Activity 3 to check whether the expenses incurred are reasonable.

Additional Idea: *When suggesting how the business performance can be improved, you may introduce the verbs describing cause and effect.*

> have a positive impact
> affect
> cause
> lead to
> result in
> consequently
> as a consequence
> due to

Example: *Finding cheaper premises might have a considerable impact on your net earnings.*

UNIT 6

EXTRA ACTIVITY 1: The Key

ASSETS	LIABILITIES
Current Assets	**Current Liabilities**
cash and cash equivalents	short-term borrowings
accounts receivable	accounts payable
prepaid expenses	accrued expenses
marketable securities	insurance liability
inventories	dividends payable
Non-Current Assets	**Non-Current Liabilities**
property, plant and equipment	long-term borrowings
government securities	
Intangible Assets	
goodwill	
trademarks	
Total Assets:	**Total Liabilities:**
Shareholders' Equity:	

UNIT 7

EXTRA ACTIVITY 2: Possible Solutions

- ask customers for cash on delivery
- reduce credit terms
- add penalty charges for late payment
- ask supplier for extended payment terms
- reduce inventory to a minimum
- find cheaper suppliers
- cut the staff wage bill
- reduce the time for making product / providing services
- increase prices
- increase sales

EXTRA ACTIVITY 3: The Key

1. **Opening Balance** is the amount at the beginning of accounting period.
2. **Closing Balance** is the amount at the end of accounting period.
3. **Share Capital** (**US: Common Stock**) is the amount of money that a company received in exchange for company shares.
4. **Retained Earnings** represent the amount of the net income retained by a company for reinvestment in its operations and not distributed in form of dividends.
5. **Dividends** represent the amount of net earnings distributed to shareholders proportional to the number of shares owned.
6. **Par Value (Nominal Value)** is the price of shares at which they were initially issued by a company, unrelated to its market price.
7. **Additional Paid-In Capital** is the value of a company's shares that is above the value at which they were initially issued.
8. **Treasury shares** (**US: Treasury Stock**) are shares bought back or held by a company.
9. **Unrealised Gain or Loss** is a gain (or loss) that exists on paper and is not realised until the underlying asset is sold.
10. **Comprehensive Income** is the sum of net income and other items that are not recognised in income statement because they have not been realised.

UNIT 9

EXTRA ACTIVITY 1

Pair work: Students interview each other in order to complete the Invoice.

Note: 'Ship to' refers to location where the goods are shipped. 'Bill to' is the location where the invoice is sent for the goods that have been shipped.

UNIT 10

EXTRA ACTIVITY 1: The Key

1. The owner of a company personally acquires an office building and rents the space in it to his company at $ 5,000 per month.

   Business entity principle: *The amount is recorded in company records as a valid expense, whereas for the owner the amount is taxable income.*

2. An item in inventory has a cost of $ 20, but it can be replaced for $ 15.

   Conservatism principle: *An accountant reports the item in inventory at $ 15 and the loss of $ 5.*

3. A company is involved in a lawsuit, which it is likely to lose.

   Conservatism principle: *An accountant records a contingent liability.*

4. A company is involved in a lawsuit, which it is likely to win.

   Conservatism principle: *As an accountant cannot anticipate gains, the potential gain is not reported.*

5. You are an accountant. Your client claims he had a receipt for a purchase he made, but he is unable to find it.

   Objectivity principle: *An accountant will not record the purchase as a valid expense because of lack of objective evidence.*

6. A company has net assets worth $ 10 million. Customer A, who owes $ 1,000 to the Company X, defaults.

   Relevance principle: *The information is immaterial to the company's financial statements and it will not be included.*

7. Under a bonus plan, an employee earns a $10,000 bonus based on measurable aspects of his performance within the current year. The bonus is paid in the following year.

   Matching principle: *The bonus is recorded within the year when the employee earned it.*

8. A company is exhibiting indicators such as defaulting on its loans, incurring significant trading losses, has a rising level of short-term overdrafts not supported by operational growth. In addition, it faces a number of legal proceedings. The company is undergoing an audit.

   Going concern principle: *An auditor should express his doubts about the entity's ability to continue as a going concern.*

9. The tax rate is expected to change in near future.

   Full disclosure principle: *The information should be included in financial statements.*

UNIT 11

EXTRA ACTIVITY 1: The Key

1. Contracting officers were accused of accepting money in return for steering multi-million dollar contracts to certain companies.
   BRIBERY

2. An employee of a financial institution diverted funds from legitimate accounts into "dummy" accounts.
   EMBEZZLEMENT

3. An accounts payable clerk used her computer to access the company's accounting software without authorisation and issued various cheques payable to himself and others.
   EMBEZZLEMENT; FRAUD;

4. A company's false financial reporting caused a subsequent loss to investors amounting to US$11 billion.
   FALSIFICATION; FRAUD;

5. A town mayor used public funds to build his private house.
   MISAPPROPRIATION

6. A customer was invoiced for 100 boxes, but only 98 actually arrived.
   SHORT-SHIPMENT

7. A film star has been caught 'borrowing' items from a shop.
   SHOPLIFTING

8. An employee has been caught taking stamps and paper from work.
   PILFERING

9. A company published a book without paying for the copyrights.
   COPYRIGHT INFRINGEMENT

10. A corporate manager sold an overseas corporate real estate asset at a fraction of its market value to a front company that he owned.
    FRAUD

UNIT 11

EXTRA ACTIVITY 2: The Key

Match the accounting fraud to the area it is related to:

| accounts receivable | inventory |
| liability and expense | assets |

1. not recording customer warranty claims: **liability and expense**
2. recording fictitious revenues (related parties, consignment or sham sales): **accounts receivable**
3. not writing off uncollectable debts: **accounts receivable**
4. manipulating cash received from related parties as cash received from customers: **accounts receivable**
5. overvaluation of finished goods: **inventory**
6. not recording contingent liabilities: **liability and expense**
7. not writing off obsolete stock items: **inventory**
8. overstating assets through mergers and acquisitions: **overstating assets**
9. recording fictitious inventory into the books of accounts: **accounts receivable**
10. not recording accounts payable: **liability and expense**
11. understating provision for doubtful debts: **liability and expense**
12. overstating marketable securities: **assets**
13. failing to record depreciation / amortisation expense: **liability and expense**
14. under-recording purchases: **inventory**
15. over-counting physical inventory: **inventory**
16. not recording accrued expense: **liability and expense**

UNIT 11

EXTRA ACTIVITY 3: Suggested Answers

1. **Control over information processing:** checking of data entered; controlling access to data files and programmes
2. **Segregation of duties:** dividing key duties and responsibilities among different people to reduce the risk of error or fraud
3. **Access restriction to resources and records:** access limited to authorised individuals and their accountability should be assigned and maintained
4. **Physical control over vulnerable assets:** limited access to assets such as cash, securities, inventory and equipment, requiring a second signature on cash disbursement
5. **Reconciliation:** performing physical inventory counts, reconciling purchase orders, invoices and bank statements, comparing inventory changes to amounts purchased and sold
6. **Inspection of incoming shipment before making payment to suppliers:** a careful inspection prevents short-shipment and other similar manipulations
7. **Appropriate documentation of transactions:** documentation should be properly managed, maintained and readily available for examination

UNIT 12

EXTRA ACTIVITY 1: The Key

1. A company pays $ 30,000 rent payment in December for the period from January to June of the following year: **deferred expense**

2. A restaurant paid an annual franchise fee in October 2017 for the following year: **deferred expense**

3. An IT maintenance company repaired a customer's computer two months ago. The customer paid the invoice by the end of next month: **deferred revenue**

4. Financial News Magazine sells subscription to their magazine, which is published 12 times a year. The annual subscription costs $ 250: **deferred revenue**

5. In 2017, a company buys a lorry for $ 12,000. They expect the lorry to last 5 years. The company records an annual depreciation expense at $ 2,000: **deferred expense**

6. A company received a rent payment for the next six months' occupancy: **deferred revenue**

7. A company paid advertising costs for the campaign that will last 6 months: **deferred expense**

8. In October, a company received cash in advance of rendering services. A half of the services will be provided by 31 December: **deferred revenue**

9. In May 2017, a company sold goods worth $ 5,000 on credit. It should receive the payment in the following year: **accrued revenue**

10. A company paid $ 12,000 insurance premium in December for the insurance protection for the period from January to June of the following year: **deferred expense**

UNIT 13

EXTRA ACTIVITY 1: The Key

1. **Case Study 1:**
   Students provide their own estimates with respect to the estimated residual value, depreciable amount and depreciation rate.

   useful life: 10 years
   historical cost: $ 100,000
   recovery period: 10 years

2. **Case Study 2: Straight Line Method**
   Depreciation expense: $ 250
   Calculated as follows:
   Depreciable amount: $ 1,500 (2,000-500)
   Annual depreciation expense: $ 500 (1,500÷3)
   Depreciation expense for 6 months, i.e. from 1 January to 30 June: $ 250

3. **Case Study 3: Accelerated Method**
   Depreciation expense in the first year: $4,000 (40% of $ 10,000)
   Depreciation expense in the remaining four years: $1,500
   Calculated as follows: 10,000 - 4,000=6,000
   6,000 ÷ 4=1,500

EXTRA ACTIVITY 2: Causes of Depreciation

Work with a partner. Describe a situation illustrating one of the causes of depreciation listed below. Your partner should guess what you are describing.

Wear and Tear
Deterioration
Obsolescence
Inadequacy *
Depletion of Natural Resources**

Inadequacy arises when an asset is no longer used because of growth and changes in the size of the business
**Some assets are of wasting nature, as a result of extraction of mineral resources or raw materials from them*

UNIT 14

EXTRA ACTIVITY 1: The Key

Question 1: You file an application for a patent
Question 2: You file a design registration
Question 3: You file an application for a trademark
Question 4: You file an application for a copyright registration
Question 5: Trademark Infringement
Question 6: Customer list
Question 7: Goodwill
Question 8: Royalty

UNIT 15

EXTRA ACTIVITY 1: The Key

1. spends time getting to know the business, as well as the environment and the industry in which it operates
   (EXTERNAL)

2. analyses the internal business and financial systems used to make and record transactions
   (INTERNAL)

3. gathers evidence on the business methods and transactions of the company
   (EXTERNAL)

4. gives advice on the business methods and transactions of the company
   (INTERNAL)

5. examines financial statements to determine whether they conform to relevant accounting principles
   (EXTERNAL)

6. examines the management report and determines whether it conforms to the financial statements
   (EXTERNAL)

7. guarantees the correctness of the figures presented in the accounts
   (INTERNAL)

8. provides consulting services
   (INTERNAL)

9. presents a written report to the management of the company, describing whether the accounting records, financial statements and management reports conform to legal requirements
   (EXTERNAL)

10. maintains confidentiality and independence
    (EXTERNAL)

COLLOCATION BANK

Essential Noun-Verb Combinations

A

ACCOUNT
    verb + account: audit; credit to; debit to; check; keep; inspect; maintain; reconcile; update;

ACCOUNTS RECEIVABLE
    verb + accounts receivable: audit; collect; record; report;

ACCOUNTS PAYABLE
    verb + accounts payable: audit; settle; record; report;

ACCOUNTING POLICY:
    verb + accounting policy: adopt; apply; create; design; implement; review;
    accounting policy + verb: be aimed at;

ADJUSTING ENTRY
    verb + adjusting entry: make; post; record;

ASSESSMENT
    verb + assessment: carry out; perform; undertake;

ASSET
    verb + asset: acquire; dispose of; own; record; report; possess; realise;

AUDIT
    verb + audit: conduct; perform; carry out; undergo; undertake;

B

BALANCE
    verb + balance: calculate; carry forward; carry over; credit; debit; reconcile; transfer;
    balance + verb: be in agreement;

C

COST
    verb + cost: allocate; bear; calculate; cover; estimate; incur; increase; meet; reduce; reimburse;

CRIME
    verb + crime: commit; combat; cut; deter; investigate; perpetrate; prevent; reduce; tackle;

D

DEDUCTION
    verb + deduction: make; subtract;

DEPRECIATION
    verb + depreciation: calculate; charge;

E

ENTRY
    verb + entry: cancel; post; record; transfer;

EXPENSE
    verb + expense: bear; charge; debit; deduct; incur; meet; record; report;
    expense + verb: arise; be offset against;

F

FINANCIAL STATEMENTS
    verb + financial statements: analyse; audit; compile; examine; inspect; prepare;
    financial statements + verb: disclose; report;

FINANCIAL RECORDS
    verb + financial records: audit; check; examine; inspect; keep; maintain; prepare; review;

FRAUD
    verb + fraud: combat; commit; perpetrate; prevent;

G

GAIN
    verb + gain: earn; generate; record; report;
    gain + verb: arise;

GOODS
    verb + goods: deliver; manufacture; produce; sell;

I

INCOME
    income + verb: earn; distribute; generate; record; report; yield;

INVOICE
    verb + invoice: issue; inspect; pay; receive; send;

INTERNAL CONTROL
verb + internal control: design; improve; inspect; lack of; monitor; review; test;
internal control + verb: involve; be aimed at;

IMPAIRMENT
verb + impairment: test for;

ITEM
verb + item: eliminate; offset; post; record; write off;

L

LAW
verb + law: adopt; comply with; enact; interpret; observe; pass; violate;
law + verb: govern; prescribe; stipulate;

LEDGER
verb + ledger: maintain; record in;

LIABILITY
verb + liability: assume; discharge; incur; meet; settle;

LOSS
verb + loss: disclose; incur; offset; record; report; sustain;

M

MEASURE
verb + measure: adopt; design; implement; impose; introduce;
measure + verb: be aimed at; be designed to; be intended to;

P

PAYROLL
verb + payroll: administer; be on; calculate;

POLICY
verb + policy: adopt; design; develop; follow; formulate; implement; outline; pursue;
policy + verb: be aimed at;

PROCEDURE
verb + policy: adopt; design; establish; follow; implement; monitor; outline; scrutinise;

PRINCIPLE
verb + principle: adopt; apply; establish; formulate;
principle + verb: apply; prescribe; state; underlie;

PROFIT
verb + profit: earn; generate; disclose; make; record; report;

R

REVENUE
    verb + revenue: earn; generate; produce; yield;

S

SECURITIES
    verb + securities: buy; issue; sell; trade;

SERVICE
    verb + service: improve; provide; render;
    service + verb: improve; deteriorate;

STRATEGY
    verb + strategy: adopt; create; design; develop; devise; employ; implement;

T

TAX
    verb + tax: calculate; charge; collect; deduct; impose; introduce; levy; be exempt from; withhold;

TAX EVASION
    verb + tax evasion: commit; combat; perpetrate; prevent;

TAX RETURN
    verb + tax return: complete; fill in; file; lodge; submit;

TRANSACTION
    verb + transaction: enter; post; record.

GLOSSARY

A

accelerated method: the method of calculating depreciation in which more rapid depreciation occurs at the beginning of an asset's useful life instead of being spread out equally over a number of years

accountability: an obligation or willingness to accept responsibility

accounting cycle: a series of steps in recording an accounting event from the time a transaction occurs to its inclusion in financial statements

accounts payable: money that a company owes to its suppliers

accounting policy: principles, rules and procedures selected, and consistently followed, by the management of an organisation in preparing and reporting the financial statements

accounting principles: rules and guidelines that guide the preparation of financial statements

accounts receivable: money owed to a company by its debtors

accrual basis accounting: a method of recording accounting transactions for revenue when earned and expenses when incurred

accrued expense: an expense recognised in the books before it is paid for

acquisition: a purchase of one business entity by another

acquisition price: original purchase price

additional paid-in capital: any payment received from investors for stock that exceeds the par value of the stock

adhere (verb): conform to or follow the rules

adjusting entry: a journal entry made at the end of the accounting period to allocate revenue and expenses to the period in which they actually are applicable

adjusted trial balance: a list of balances of ledger accounts created after the adjusting entries are made and posted to ledger accounts

advance payment: a prepayment

adverse opinion: an auditor's opinion that contains a major exception or warning

allocation of costs: the process of identifying and assigning costs to cost objects

amortisation: a decrease in value of an intangible asset

anomalous entry: irregular, abnormal entry

approximation: a close guess of the actual value

asset: any item of economic value owned by an individual or business entity

assumption: a statement that is presumed to be true without concrete evidence to support it

assurance: 1. certainty about something 2. a high-level review of financial statements

B

balance sheet: a financial report that summarises an entity's assets, liabilities and shareholders' equity at a specific point in time

bank statement: a bank report that summarises all transactions

book value (carrying value): the amount at which an asset or liability is recognised in financial accounting

Glossary

bookkeeper: a person who is responsible for processing the records of a company's financial activities
business combination: a transaction in which the acquirer obtains control of another business
brand recognition: the extent to which a consumer can identify a particular product or service
bribery: offering money to someone in return for a favour
business premises: the buildings or land owned or used by a business organisation
bypass (verb): ignore

C

capital gains tax: a tax levied on profit from the sale of property or of an investment
carry forward (verb): move to a later accounting period
cash disbursement: payment of money to settle obligations to accounts payable
cash flow statement: a financial report that provides an overview of a company's cash inflows and outflows
cash inflow: money received by a company as a result of its business activities
cash outflow: money paid out by a company as a result of its business activities
cash receipt: a proof of purchase issued when the buyer has paid in cash
cash register: a mechanical device for registering and calculating transactions at a point of sale
certified public accountant: in the USA, a person who has passed a professional examination administered by the American Institute of Certified Public Accountants
chart of accounts: a listing of all accounts used in the general ledger of a company
chartered accountant: in the UK, an accountant who has passed professional examination and obtained a licence
clerical error: a minor, unintentional mistake in computing figures or recording transactions
closing balance: the amount remaining in an account at the end of an accounting period
closing entry: a journal entry made at the end of an accounting period to transfer the temporary account balances to the permanent accounts
closing the books: transferring balances from temporary accounts to a permanent account
common stock (ordinary shares): securities representing equity ownership in a company
company registration number: a unique number issued when a company is incorporated
competitive intangible assets: assets that generate competitive advantage
compliance: being in conformity with laws
comply with (verb): to act in accordance with rules
confidentiality of information: a set of rules that limit access to certain types of information
conservatism: in accounting, making sure that assets and income are not overstated and liabilities and expenses are not understated
consolidated income statement: a combined income statement of a parent company with its subsidiaries
contingent liability: a potential liability depending on the outcome of a future event
controller (comptroller): a head of the accounting department
cooking the books: falsification of accounting records to give a misleading picture of a firm's financial position
copyright: the exclusive right to reproduce, publish, sell or distribute something
corporate accountant: an internal company accountant

corporate income tax: a direct tax levied by the government on profits of a company

correcting entry: a journal entry made in order to correct an erroneous amount previously entered in the general ledger

cost: the amount of cash paid to acquire a product

cost allocation: the process of identifying and assigning costs to cost objects

cost-approach: the approach based on the cost required to create or recreate a similar intangible asset

cost model: under the cost model, after initial recognition, an intangible asset is carried at its cost less any subsequent accumulated amortisation and impairment losses

cost of goods sold: total of all costs use to create a product or service

creative accounting: the exploitation of loopholes in financial regulations in order to gain advantage or present figures in a misleadingly favourable light

credit entry: an accounting entry that either increases a liability or decreases an asset

current assets: assets that are easily converted into cash within one year

current liabilities: a debt due within a year

customs duty: a tax charged by customs authorities on merchandise imported or exported from one country to another

D

date of maturity: the date when an invoice must be paid

debit entry: an accounting entry that results in either an increase in assets or decrease in liabilities

debt-to-equity ratio: total liabilities divided by shareholders' equity

deduct (verb): subtract or take away an amount

default: a situation when a debtor is unable to pay a debt

defer (verb): postpone to a later time

delinquent accounts: accounts that are past due

depletion: a reduction in the quantity of something

deposit slip (paying-in slip): a paper slip used to deposit funds into a bank account

depreciation: reduction in the value of an asset with the passage of time

derecognition: removal of an item from a balance sheet

deterrent: a thing that discourages someone from doing something

direct costs: costs associated with the product being manufactured

direct labour: the cost of paying workers who are directly involved in production of goods or supplying services

direct material: raw materials that become part of the finished product

direct tax: a tax paid directly to the government

disclaimer of opinion: an auditor's statement disclaiming any opinion regarding the company's financial position due to lack of information

disclose (verb): to make a *company or individual's* financial information available

disclosures: material facts disclosed in financial statements

discontinued operation: a segment of a company's business that has been sold, disposed of or abandoned

discrepancy: a difference between the things that should be the same

disposal: giving up ownership of an asset by sale, exchange, transfer, abandonment, etc.
dividend: a share of the after-tax profit of a company, distributed to its shareholders
double-entry bookkeeping: an accounting system in which each transaction is recorded in at least two accounts: one account is debited and the other account is credited

E

earnings per share: a company's net income divided by the number of its outstanding shares
embezzlement: stealing money from one's employer
emphasis of matter: a paragraph in an auditor's report used to draw users' attention to important piece of information that can help understand financial statements better
employee benefits: non-cash compensations
enforced collection: collecting money from debtors using legal tools
entrepreneur: an owner of a business enterprise, who takes initiative and risks in order to earn profit
entry: a written record of a transaction
excise duty: an indirect tax on the sale or use of specific products, usually applied as an amount per quantity of the product
estimate: a rough calculation of something
expense: a part of the cost used to generate revenue
expert witness: a person permitted to testify at a trial because of special knowledge in a particular field relevant to the case

F

fair value: the market value of an asset
falsification: changing figures, records, etc. so that they contain false information
fictitious: false, invented in order to deceive or mislead
financial audit: an independent, objective evaluation of a company's financial records and reporting activities
financial records: financial documents representing transactions of a company
financial statements: a collection of reports describing a company's financial results, financial position and cash flows
fixed asset: an asset that is not consumed or sold during the normal course of business
fixed costs: costs that remain the same regardless of the level of production
foreign currency translation: conversion of currency
forensic accountant: an accountant whose job is to examine financial records in order to detect possible fraudulent activities
forgery: making a false signature or document to make people think that it is real
franchise: the licence to sell a company's product or service in a particular area
fraud: doing something illegal in order to get money
fraudulent: dishonest and illegal
fundamental analysis: an evaluation of a company's stock based on the examination of a company's financial statements

G

gain: any economic benefit derived outside the normal operations of a company
general partnership: a type of business where both partners share profits and liabilities equally
gearing (leverage): the amount of money a company has borrowed compared to its share capital
go public (verb): to sell shares on a stock market for the first time
going concern: the assumption that an entity will remain in business for the foreseeable future
goodwill: part of a *company's* value that includes things that cannot be directly measured, for example, its good reputation or its customers' loyalty
gross earnings: the total income of an individual earned in a year, as calculated prior to any tax deductions or adjustments
gross margin: the difference between the total revenue and cost of goods sold

H

historical cost: the original cost incurred to acquire an asset
holding company: a company that controls other companies through stock ownership but that usually does not engage directly in their productive operations
human capital: the skills, knowledge and experience that employees acquire on the job

I

impairment: a decline in the value of an asset below its carrying value
impropriety: something improper or unacceptable
integrity: honesty and ability to do what is morally right
International Financial Reporting Standards: a set of generally accepted accounting principles used to prepare financial statements
income-oriented approach: the approach based on future income streams expected from the use of an intangible asset
income statement: a financial document that summarises a company's revenue and expenses for a fiscal year
income tax payable: a balance sheet account that reports taxes that must be paid within a year
incorporated entity: a business organisation that is a separate legal entity from its owners
incur (verb): to acquire, usually something negative; for example losses, costs, liability, expense
indirect costs: costs that are not directly related to making a product or service
indirect tax: a tax paid by consumers when they buy goods or services
infringement: a violation of a law, agreement, etc.
inheritance tax: a tax imposed on someone who inherits property or money
insider trading: the illegal practice of trading on the stock exchange to one's own advantage through having access to confidential information
intangible asset: a non-physical asset having a useful life greater than one year
inventory: stock
invoice: an itemised bill for goods sold or services provided

J

journal: a book in which transactions are first recorded

L

ledger: a company's main accounting records
legal entity: a business organisation that is legally permitted to enter into a contract
legal intangible assets: intangible assets that are defensible in a court
liable: legally responsible for
liability for debts: responsibility for debts
liability: financial obligation
limited partnership: a business organisation with both general and limited partners
liquid: easily convertible into cash
liquidation: the process of selling off all the assets of an entity and closing it down as a legal entity
loss: occurs when an asset is sold for a price lower than the original purchase price

M

mandatory: compulsory, obligatory
manufacturing costs: costs of all resources consumed in the process of making a product
manufacturing overheads: indirect factory-related costs that are incurred when a product is manufactured
market-price approach: the approach based on the market value of similar assets
marketable securities: securities that can be easily converted to cash
match (verb): to find a counterpart, pair
maternity leave: a period of absence from work granted to a mother before and after the birth of her child
maturity date: the date when a debt instrument becomes due for settlement
merger: a process in which at least two companies combine to form one single company
material: in accounting, an item is material if it could influence the economic decisions of users of financial statements
material adjustment: correction of a fundamental error
material misstatement: accidental or intentional untrue financial statement information that influences company's value or price of stock
mishandling: careless or incorrect handling
misleading: making someone believe something that is untrue
misrepresentation: false or misleading representation of something
money laundering: the crime of creating the appearance that money obtained from illegal activities originated from a legitimate source
mortgage loan: a loan to finance the purchase of property, where the property itself serves as collateral
municipal tax: a tax imposed by local governments (municipalities) to fund local government services

Glossary

N

net income (net earnings, bottom line): net profit

non-core activities: peripheral, secondary activities

non-current assets: assets that are purchased for long-term use and not likely to be converted quickly into cash

non-current liabilities: a debt due after a year

non-manufacturing costs: cost incurred in carrying out a company's day-to-day activities, but not directly associated with production

non-operating expenses: expenses incurred for reasons not related to a company's normal business operations

non-operating revenue: income earned through a company's non-core activities

notes to financial statements: additional information added to the end of financial statements to help explain specific items

O

objectivity: the state of being impartial and fair

obsolescence: a loss in value due to development of improved or superior equipment, but not due to physical deterioration

obsolete: no longer appropriate for the purpose it was obtained because something better has been invented

offset against (verb): to cancel each other out

opening balance: balance brought forward at the beginning of an accounting period

operating cash flow ratio: cash flow from operations divided by current liabilities

operating expenses: expenses incurred from primary activities

operating margin: gross margin minus selling, general and administrative expenses

operating revenue: revenue earned from primary activities

outstanding invoice: an unpaid invoices that is not yet due

outstanding share: a company's shares currently held by all its shareholders

overdue invoice: a past due invoice

overstate (verb): to say that something that is larger or greater than it really is

owner's equity: the owner's share of the assets of a company

P

patent: legal protection of an idea or invention

payroll: a financial record of employees' salaries, wages, bonuses, net pay and deductions

payroll tax: a tax levied against the amount of wages and salaries paid to workers

payslip: a slip of paper given to an employee when they have been paid, detailing the amount of pay given and the tax and insurance deducted

permanent accounts: accounts that are not closed at the end of an accounting period

personal income tax: a direct tax imposed by the government on a person's annual income
pervasive: widespread
predominant activity: the main company's activity
physical inventory count: a process where a company physically counts its entire inventory
physical deterioration: a decline in physical condition
private limited company: a limited liability company whose shares are not sold on stock exchange
procurement: purchasing
professional scepticism: a critical attitude assumed by auditors during an audit
property tax: a tax levied on property
public accountant: an accountant whose services are available to public at large
purchase order: a company document sent to vendors by the purchasing department
purchase requisition form: a company document used to initiate a purchase

Q

qualified opinion: an auditor's opinion stating that financial statements are fairly presented, except for a specified issue

R

random sampling: a method of selecting a sample where each member of a group has an equal likelihood of selection
relevance: in accounting, relevance means it will make a difference to a decision-maker
remuneration: a general term that describes all forms of payment for work that has been done or services provided
render services: provide services
restatement of financial statements: revision of a company's previous financial statements when it is determined that it contained a material inaccuracy
retained earnings: the percentage of net earnings not paid out as dividends, but retained by the company to be reinvested in its core business, or to pay debt
revaluation model: under the revaluation model, after an initial recognition, an intangible asset is carried at a revalued amount, less any subsequent accumulated amortisation and impairment losses

S

safeguard (verb): protect
salary: a fixed regular payment
salvage value: the expected or estimated value of an asset at the end of its useful life
scope paragraph: a paragraph containing a description of the work the auditor performed
securities: a financial or investment instrument that can be traded on financial markets
self-employed: working for oneself rather than for an employer
shareholders (stockholder): a person who owns shares in a company and is entitled to a part of its profit

Glossary

shareholders' equity: the amount of a company's assets owned by its shareholders

short-shipment: a situation when the quantity of cargo received is less than the quantity listed in documents

sick pay: money given by an employer to someone who cannot work because of illness

social security contributions: compulsory payments paid to government to receive a future social benefit

sole proprietorship: an unincorporated business owned by one person who has a complete control over business affairs

source document: a record of financial transaction

stakeholder: 1. an interested party 2. a person owning shares in a company

stamp duty land tax (transfer tax): a tax levied on purchase of houses, flats, and other land and building

statement of changes in equity: a financial statement telling the users about the value of equity at the beginning of an accounting period and how it has changed during a year

statutory: legally required

straight- line method: the method of calculating depreciation in which amount of depreciation charged over an asset's useful life remains the same

stock exchange: a market in which securities are traded

subsidiary: a daughter company

T

tax allowance: a part of income which a person is allowed to earn and not pay tax on

tax base: the amount to which a tax rate is applied to calculate the tax owed

tax compliance: willingness to obey tax laws

tax credit: a) a tax incentive which allows certain taxpayers to subtract the amount of the credit from the amount of tax owed b) prepaid income tax that can be offset against the total income tax payable

tax deduction: the amount subtracted from the gross income when calculating taxable income

tax due-diligence report: an audit aimed at identifying tax risks of a transaction

tax evasion: an illegal non-payment or underpayment of tax liability

tax exemption: relief from taxes

tax identification number (unique taxpayer reference): an identifying number used for tax purposes

tax liability: the total amount of tax that a person or organisation must pay

tax optimisation: a process that involves searching for and identifying the legal and other means to ensure the lowest possible level of taxation for an entity or individual

tax rate: tax liability expressed as a percentage of taxable income

tax refund: the return by the government of the difference between taxes paid and taxes owed

tax relief: a reduction in tax liability allowed for a particular reason

tax return: a statement on an official form showing income, deductions, exemptions, and taxes due

taxable income: the amount of income subject to income tax

temporary account: a general ledger account that begins each accounting year with a zero balance

tenant: a person who pays rent for the use of premises

terms of payment: conditions of payment agreed between a buyer and seller

threshold: the level at which something starts to happen or have effect

Glossary

timing differences: the differences between the transaction event and the transfer of cash

trademark: a name, symbol or design that a company uses for its product and that cannot be used by anyone else

transaction: any business event that affects the financial position of a company

transfer pricing: a price of transactions between controlled (or related) legal entities

transparent: of information: visible and accessible

treasury shares: a company's own repurchased shares

U

unadjusted trial balance: a listing of general ledger account balances at the end of a reporting period, before any adjusting entries are made

understate (verb): to say that something is smaller than it really is

unemployment insurance: funds paid by the state to unemployed workers who have lost their jobs due to layoffs

unincorporated entity: an entity with no legal difference between the owner and the entity

unqualified opinion: an auditor's opinion stating that financial statements present a fair and accurate picture of a company and comply with the relevant accounting principles.

useful life: the length of time an asset is expected to be usable for the purpose it was acquired

utilities: services such as electricity, telephone, water supply provided to the public

V

value added tax: a tax on the amount by which the value of an article has been increased at each stage of its production or distribution

variable costs: cost that change with the level of production

verifiable: capable of being verified

verification: use of tests to ensure the accuracy or truth of information

W

wage: a payment based on number of hours an employee worked

wear and tear: damage or deterioration resulting from ordinary use

white-collar crime: a nonviolent crime committed for financial gain

working capital ratio: current assets minus current liabilities

withholding tax: that part of an employee's tax liability withheld by the employer from wages or salary and paid directly to the government

write off: a cancellation of an asset from a balance sheet

Y

year-end closing procedures: a set of activities aimed at preparing accounts for the coming year